Euripides: Hecuba

COMPANIONS TO GREEK AND ROMAN TRAGEDY

Series Editor: Thomas Harrison

Aeschylus: Agamemnon Barbara Goward
Aeschylus: Eumenides Robin Mitchell-Boyask
Aeschylus: Persians David Rosenbloom
Aeschylus: Prometheus Bound I. A. Ruffell
Aeschylus: Seven Against Thebes Isabelle Torrance
Aeschylus: Suppliants Thalia Papadopoulou
Euripides: Alcestis Niall W. Slater
Euripides: Bacchae Sophie Mills
Euripides: Heracles Emma Griffiths
Euripides: Hippolytus Sophie Mills
Euripides: Ion Laura Swift
Euripides: Iphigenia at Aulis Pantelis Michelakis
Euripides: Medea William Allan
Euripides: Orestes Matthew Wright
Euripides: Phoenician Women Thalia Papadopoulou
Euripides: Suppliant Women Ian Storey
Euripides: Trojan Women Barbara Goff
Seneca: Phaedra Roland Mayer
Seneca: Thyestes Peter Davis
Sophocles: Ajax Jon Hesk
Sophocles: Electra Michael Lloyd
Sophocles: Oedipus at Colonus Adrian Kelly
Sophocles: Philoctetes Hanna Roisman
Sophocles: Women of Trachis Brad Levett

Euripides: Hecuba

Helene P. Foley

BLOOMSBURY
LONDON · NEW DELHI · NEW YORK · SYDNEY

Bloomsbury Academic
An imprint of Bloomsbury Publishing Plc

50 Bedford Square	1385 Broadway
London	New York
WC1B 3DP	NY 10018
UK	USA

www.bloomsbury.com

BLOOMSBURY and the Diana logo are trademarks of Bloomsbury Publishing Plc

First published 2015

© 2015 Helene P. Foley

Helene P. Foley has asserted her right under the Copyright, Designs and Patents Act, 1988, to be identified as Author of this work.

All rights reserved. No part of this publication may be reproduced or transmitted in any form or by any means, electronic or mechanical, including photocopying, recording, or any information storage or retrieval system, without prior permission in writing from the publishers.

No responsibility for loss caused to any individual or organization acting on or refraining from action as a result of the material in this publication can be accepted by Bloomsbury Academic or the author.

British Library Cataloguing-in-Publication Data
A catalogue record for this book is available from the British Library.

ISBN: HB: 978-1-47256-907-3
PB: 978-1-47256-906-6
ePub: 978-1-47256-908-0
ePDF: 978-1-47256-909-7

Library of Congress Cataloging-in-Publication Data
Foley, Helene P., 1942– author.
Euripides, Hecuba / by Helene P. Foley.
   pages cm
Includes bibliographical references and index.
ISBN 978-1-4725-6907-3 (hardback) — ISBN 978-1-4725-6906-6 (pbk.)
1. Euripides. Hecuba. 2. Greek drama—History and criticism.   I. Title.
 PA3973.H3F65 2014
 882'.01—dc23
 2014017407

Typeset by RefineCatch Limited, Bungay, Suffolk

Contents

Maps of the World of Hecuba	vii
List of Illustrations	ix
Acknowledgments	xi
Preface	xiii

1	The Play in its Context	1
2	Theatrical Festivals and the Mythical Tradition	11
	The Performance Context	11
	The Mythical Tradition	14
3	Dramatic Structure and Unity	25
	The Action of the Play	25
	The 'Problem of Unity'	29
4	Interpreting the Action: Hecuba and the Power of Persuasion	35
	Ghosts in Greek Tragedy	35
	Hecuba's Entrance	37
	The Debate between Odysseus and Hecuba	38
	Polyxena's Sacrifice	42
	Hecuba's Supplication to Agamemnon	45
5	Hecuba's Revenge	51
	The Final 'Trial'	54
	Hecuba's Trial Speech	55
6	The Role of the Chorus	61
7	Sizing up Revenge Tragedy	67
	Concluding Analysis of the Play	73

8	Performances of *Hecuba*	77
	Pre-twentieth-century Performances	77
	Twentieth- and Twenty-first-century Performances	78

Chronology	91
Glossary of Ancient and Technical Terms	103
Guide to Further Reading	107
Notes	111
Bibliography	131
Index	141

Maps of the World of Hecuba

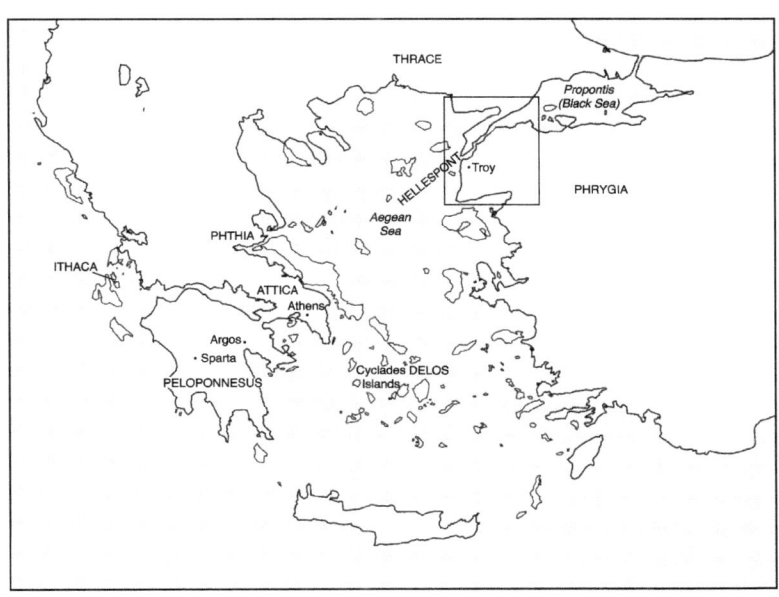

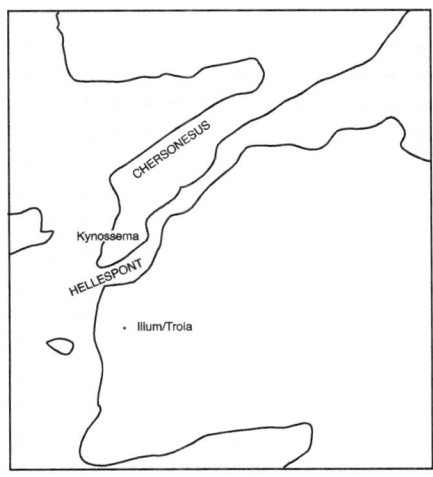

List of Illustrations

1 The Sacrifice of Polyxena, Tyrrhenian black-figure amphora by the Timiades Painter dated c. 550 BCE (British Museum, London 1897.7–27.2). 17
2, A and B Drawings based on an original by Nurten Sevinç of the sacrifice of Polyxena on two sides of a late archaic marble sarcophagus at the Çanakkale Archaeological Museum in Turkey dated c. 520–500 BCE. The circles represent small drill holes. Courtesy of the Troy Excavation Project. 19
3 Olympia Dukakis as Hekabe with the Chorus Leader, Remi Barclay Bosseau, in *Hekabe*, directed by Carey Perloff in 1995, American Conservatory Theater, Yerba Buena Center, San Francisco. Courtesy of the American Conservatory Theater. Photograph by Ken Friedman. 83
4 Clare Higgins as Hecuba in a version of *Hecuba* by Frank McGuinness based on a literal translation by Fionnuala Murphy, directed in 2004 by Jonathan Kent at the Donmar Warehouse, London, England. 87

Acknowledgments

I would like to thank Rachel Kitzinger for her careful reading of this manuscript, Charlotte Loveridge and Anna MacDiarmid for facilitating this manuscript, and Dave Prout for the index.

Preface

Hecuba emerged as one of the ten canonical plays by Euripides during the Hellenistic period in Greece; the play was popular throughout Antiquity and became part of the so-called 'Byzantine triad' of three plays of Euripides (along with *Phoenician Women* and *Orestes*) selected for study in school curricula, above all for the brilliance of its rhetorical speeches and quotable traditional wisdom. Both translations into Latin and vernacular languages and stage performances emerged early in the sixteenth century. The Renaissance admired the play for its representation of the extraordinary suffering and misfortunes of its newly enslaved heroine, the former queen of Troy Hecuba, for the courageous sacrificial death of her daughter Polyxena, and for the beleaguered queen's surprisingly successful revenge against the unscrupulous killer of her son Polydorus. Later periods, however, developed reservations about the play's revenge plot and its purported lack of unity. Recent scholarship has favorably reassessed the play in its original cultural and political context and the past thirty years have generated a number of exciting staged productions. *Hecuba* has emerged as a profound exploration of the difficulties of establishing justice and a stable morality in post-war situations. This book will investigate the play's changing critical and theatrical reception from Antiquity to the present, its mythical and political background, its dramatic and thematic unity, and the role of its choruses.

References to the Euripidean text follow James Diggle's edition in the Oxford Classical Text series (J. Diggle 1994, *Euripides Fabulae*: Tomus III). For controversial passages, several other editions have been taken into account. Translations are quoted from Christopher Collard 1991 (*Euripides Hecuba*. Warminster: Aris and Phillips) unless otherwise noted.

The following abbreviations of book titles have been used:

Davies = M. Davies (1988), *Epicorum Graecorum Fragmenta*, Göttingen: Vandenboeck and Ruprecht.

K-A = R. Kassel and C. Austin (1984), *Poetae Comici Graeci*, vol iii.2. *Aristophanes: Testimonia et Fragmenta*. Berlin and New York: Walter de Gruyter.

LIMC = *Lexicon Iconographicum Mythologiae Classicae* (9 volumes in 18 parts, 1981–99). Zurich and Munich: Artemis Verlag.

PMG = D. Page (ed.) (1962), *Poetae Melici Graeci*. Oxford: Oxford University Press.

PMGF = M. Davies (1991), *Poetarum Melicorum Graecorum Fragmenta*. Oxford: Oxford University Press.

Snell = B. Snell (1964), *Pindari Carmina cum Fragmentis*. Leipzig: Teubner.

TrGF = R. Kannicht (2004), *Tragicorum Graecorum Fragmenta*, vol. 5: *Euripides*. Göttingen: Vandenboeck and Ruprecht.

Information about modern productions of Euripides' Hecuba is available on-line from two databases: The Archive of Performances of Greek and Roman Drama (Oxford University, www.apgrd.ox.ac.uk) and The Reception of Texts and Images of Ancient Greece in Late Twentieth-Century Drama and Poetry in English (The Open University, www2.open.ac.uk/ClassicalStudies/GreekPlays).

The Oxford Guide to Classical Mythology in the Arts, ed. J. D. Reid, New York: Oxford University Press provides extensive information about the reception of Hecuba and Polyxena in western art and literature.

1

The Play in its Context

In Shakespeare's *Hamlet*, Hamlet asks the leader of a group of players who have come to the court in Denmark to recite a passionate speech that he once loved about the fall of Troy. The player recites the story of the horrific death of the Trojan King Priam, mutilated at an altar by the Greek son of Achilles, Pyrrhus (Neoptolemus), during the fall of Troy, but finally bursts into tears over the anguished reaction of the Trojan Queen Hecuba to observing her husband's humiliating demise. Hamlet goes on to meditate on the player's well-simulated grief in the memorable lines: 'What's Hecuba to him or he to Hecuba/that he should weep for her?' (Act 2, Scene 2). For both Antiquity and the Renaissance, Hecuba represented the epitome of the grieving wife, mother, and victim of war who had once had riches of every kind, but then lost everything. Before Euripides' play begins, she has lost not only her husband, but her many adult sons to the Greeks. Her grandson Astyanax, son of the hero Hector, has been thrown off the walls of Troy before it was burned, and she and the remaining Trojan women have been forced to board ships for a life of slavery in Greece. Her daughter, the prophetess Cassandra, has become the slave concubine of the Greek leader Agamemnon. *Hecuba* closes with the prediction that she will be killed with him in Greece by Agamemnon's wife Clytemnestra.

In Euripides' *Hecuba*, the Greeks have halted on their way home north of Troy in Thrace because the ghost of the famous Greek hero

Achilles appeared above his tomb and demanded that Hecuba's remaining daughter Polyxena be sacrificed in his honor. After Polyxena goes to her death, Hecuba discovers that her young son, Polydorus, who had been spirited away from Troy for safety because he was too young to fight, has been killed by a Thracian guest friend Polymestor for the gold he brought with him from Troy. At this point Hecuba, the symbol of grief in Antiquity as well as in Hamlet's memory, gradually metamorphoses into her other incarnation popular in the Renaissance, a figure who was viewed with much more ambivalence in later centuries, which did not share the Renaissance taste for gory revenge tragedies. With the help of her fellow Trojan slave women, she takes revenge on the greedy murderer Polymestor, blinding her betrayer and killing his two young sons. Euripides' play closes with a puzzling prediction that Hecuba will turn into a dog and fall to her death from the masthead of Agamemnon's ship; her tomb will become a beacon for sailors. In any case, we can now see that the figure of Hecuba had a second if unspoken relevance for Shakespeare's Hamlet, the once courtly prince now hesitating to exact just revenge for his own murdered father in a hostile court.[1]

In short, the avenging Hecuba of Euripides' *Hecuba* begins the play as the quintessential female victim of war and the incarnation of grief for family and nation that she has remained up to the twenty-first century; yet she is transformed into a figure who would willingly accept slavery in order to achieve the justice that the world has denied her. The victim has, with powerful justification, become the victimizer. The play's study of Hecuba's gradual transformation into an avenger willing to kill not only the guilty Polymestor, but the king's innocent children, could not be more relevant today. The corrupting violence of war, the loss of social and economic status, and the failure to receive justice regularly turn the once civilized into terrorists and murderers. Euripides' searing play explores this transformation, and in the end, fails to locate blame in any simple fashion and offers no answers.

Three extant Euripides' plays, *Trojan Women*, *Andromache*, and *Hecuba*, to say nothing of earlier Greek epic and lyric poetry, dealt with the fate of the women of fallen Troy. In contrast to the popular 'quintessential war play', *Trojan Women*, which gives a central role to Hecuba's suffering and has been performed in response to every major war in virtually every Western country during the twentieth-twenty-first centuries, however, Euripides' *Hecuba* only began after centuries of post-renaissance neglect to receive important productions in Europe and the US starting in the 1980s. Yet in Antiquity, *Hecuba* was familiar enough to be quoted by the comic poet Aristophanes (*Clouds* 1165–6 and perhaps 718; his fragmentary *Geratydes*, 156K-A), Aristotle (*Rhetoric* 1394b 4–6), and the orator Demosthenes (18.267) soon after it was first produced.[2] Plutarch (*Moralia* 334a–b) notes that the vicious tyrant Alexander of Pherae attempted to hide his weeping over an actor's performance of the sufferings of Hecuba and Polyxena in the fourth century BCE.[3] *Hecuba* became one of the ten canonical and much copied plays of Euripides in the Hellenistic period and appears in later papyrus fragments in Egypt.[4] During the Byzantine period, it formed part of a so-called Byzantine triad of Euripides' plays that also included his *Orestes* and *Phoenician Women*. Although these three plays may well have been singled out for their educational value, due to their powerful rhetorical speeches and quotable references to traditional wisdom, revenge themes are also central in different ways to all three of them.[5] Latin authors such as Ennius, Ovid, and Seneca, and the fourth-century CE Greek author Quintus of Smyrna, among many others, offered versions that directly respond to both the suffering and violence in Euripides' play. Dante, like Ovid whom he is imitating here, memorably connected Hecuba's losses to her final metamorphosis:

> Hecuba, lost, enslaved, her heart made sore
> To see Polyxena dead and then to find
> Her Polydorus stretched upon the shore,

Was driven to such madness that she declined
To howling and barking like a dog because
The weight of the great grief had so wrenched her mind
(Inferno XXX, 13–20)[6]

Insofar as we can tell, Euripides may well have invented the revenge action of this play, if not the sacrifice of Polyxena. If so, what was at stake for him in Hecuba's horrific turn to self-help justice? In what respects does his play respond to contemporary Attic political and social issues in the mid-fifth century BCE? At the time of Euripides' *Hecuba*, which apparently dates to the late 420s BCE, the Peloponnesian War between Athens and its allies and the Spartans and their allies was probably in its earlier phases—about eight years in if *Hecuba* was performed, as seems most likely, in 424 or 423. Yet already Euripides seems to sense that, as the Greek historian Thucydides argued, war brings men's characters to a level with their fortunes (*History of the Peloponnesian War* 3.81.2). Only a few years before this play (431 BCE), the famous statesman Pericles, offering a funeral oration for the Athenian war dead, celebrated Athens as a model city for Greece (Thucydides 2.34–46). In his speech, he claims that Athens' citizens gloried in devoting their lives to their city, but had no need to legislate to preserve many fundamental civilized values because everyone respected what Pericles calls the unwritten laws. By unwritten laws he presumably means agreed upon religious or traditional values thought to be rooted in 'nature,' such as honoring the gods, respecting and taking care of parents, abstaining from murdering family members, or burying the dead. These ancestral laws were held to be common to all Greeks. Yet as the Peloponnesian War dragged on, these unwritten laws were gradually sacrificed to power, empire, and expediency. Some of these traditional values, such as burying the war dead, respecting suppliants and prisoners of war, keeping oaths and observing the laws of hospitality, had at least in the Greek imagination generally been respected as part of the informal laws of war and international relations; but now they began to be threatened. In 424 BCE, perhaps just before this play, for example, the Boeotians to Athens' north refused the Athenians a chance to bury their war dead after a battle at a place called Delium.

In the play's first scene, the ghost of Hecuba's dead son Polydorus appears to tell the audience that he has not only been killed by his family's guest friend Polymestor, but cast unburied and mutilated into the sea, where his corpse is shortly to be discovered and brought to his mother. The soul of the unburied could not find rest in the world below and remained permanently dishonored. In Book 24 of Homer's *Iliad*, the Olympian gods demand that the hero Achilles give up his revengeful refusal to surrender the body of Hector to the Trojans for burial, and in the *Odyssey*, Odysseus must retrace his steps on his journey to bury the body of his comrade Elpenor (*Odyssey* 11.51–80, 12, 8–15). Sophocles' *Antigone* and *Ajax* had already made burial of a putative traitor a central dramatic issue, a burial pointedly demanded by the gods in the former play. Indeed, Attic funeral orations and Euripides' own *Suppliant Women* celebrated Athenian willingness to go to war over the burial of the seven warriors who died fighting against Thebes.[7]

The laws of hospitality violated by Polymestor in killing Hecuba's son, like the unwritten laws mentioned above, were anything but trivial in the classical world. They formed the basis of both personal and international relations. A host, for example, was bound to protect the life, property, and welfare of his guest. In a culture where travel by both sea and land was dangerous, and where war, revolution, and politics frequently resulted in exile from one's native land, the network of relations created among guest friends in different countries was critical not only to individual survival, but to the continuity of civilized life. The bonds between guest friends were formalized by rituals, including the symbolic exchange of gifts, and guest friends could expect to be treated as close relatives.[8] Greeks believed that the gods, and above all Zeus himself, would punish those who violated the sacred bonds of hospitality. Hecuba and Priam have thus understandably counted on the inviolability of their bond of guest friendship with Polymestor to protect their son despite the defeat of Troy.

During the Peloponnesian War Athenian treatment of the citizens of defeated Greek cities became an urgent contemporary issue. In a debate in the Athenian assembly shortly before (427 BCE) Euripides' play over the fate of Mytilene, a city that Athens had captured in war, the democratic leader Cleon argues in Thucydides' *History of the Peloponnesian War* that justice and Athens' international interests are incompatible (3.47.5). Even his adversary in the debate, Diodotus, who thinks that the severe punishment of the Mytileneans that the assembly is considering (killing all the men and enslaving the rest of the inhabitants) is against Athens' interest, rules out like Cleon appeals to pity and decency or equity (3.40.1, 3.48.1). Before the war, the Athenians asserted to Sparta that 'All are entitled to praise whenever they follow human nature by ruling others and end up behaving more justly than their actual power dictated' (1.76.3).[9] Yet as the war continued, Thucydides increasingly presents situations where might prevails over right and advantage and self-interest overcome moderation, justice, pity, decency or equity, traditional laws, the rights of suppliants and the dead. The later Melian debate makes the case that justice is only possible among equals (Thucydides 5.84–11).[10] Aristocratic leaders had initially upheld some of the standards that bound them to friends and allies in other Greek cities, even when those cities had become enemies. Now aristocratic friendships across political boundaries began to be viewed as dangerous by the Athenian democracy,[11] and democratic leaders like Cleon came to advocate collective gain in a more brutal fashion against the city's enemies. Hecuba relies on these traditional ties among aristocratic leaders at the beginning of Euripides' play, yet they soon prove untrustworthy.

This gradual erosion of standards eventually imploded further. As Thucydides put it in his discussion of revolutions that began to pit democrats against aristocrats in numerous Greek cities, above all in Corcyra in 427 BCE, language itself was transformed and revenge proliferated: 'Words had to change their ordinary meaning and to take the meaning that was now given to them. Reckless audacity came to be considered the courage of an ally; prudent hesitation became specious cowardice; moderation was held to be a cloak for unmanliness; cautious plotting, was termed a justifiable means of self-defense. The advocate of extreme measures was always trustworthy; his opponent a man to be suspected. To succeed in a plot was to have a shrewd head, to divine a plot still shrewder ... Revenge was held of more account than self-preservation ... The ancient simplicity into which honor so largely entered was laughed down and disappeared ... In the confusion into which life was thrown in the cities, human nature, always rebelling against the law and now its master, gladly showed itself ungoverned in passion, above respect for justice, and the enemy of all superiority; otherwise revenge would not have been set above religion, and gain above justice ... Indeed, men too often take upon themselves in the prosecution of their revenge to set an example of doing away with those general laws to which all alike look for salvation in adversity, instead of allowing them to subsist against the day of danger when their aid may be required' (3, 82–4).[12] After Euripides presented *Hecuba*, which clearly reflects the frightening transitions of this period, a violent aristocratic coup in 411 BCE temporarily eliminated Athens' democracy itself. In this context, Hecuba's turn to self-help justice hardly looks arbitrary.

In Euripides' highly ironic plays, such traditional values, the unwritten or divine laws, are often left, for reasons this book will investigate, to be voiced and defended with remarkable eloquence by women and/or slaves like Hecuba, the very people who could not act to defend them in Athens because female citizens played no direct role in Athens' assembly, army, or justice system and slaves could only hope to be defended by their masters. In this play, standards of public policy that were supported in Athens' democratic assembly and on the battlefield shockingly confront the standards of justice that still obtained to a greater degree in private cases in the law courts and in private households, where pity, equity, and appeal to law and tradition still had a stronger place.[13] When the public world abandons civilized standards, the family or the isolated individual is often left as the last bastion to defend them. In *Hecuba*, the army's otherwise valid interest in honoring the war dead like Achilles or standing by an ally like Polymestor is defined in such a way as to omit or violate justice on the level represented in the Trojan women's concerns. Hecuba herself is reduced in the service of justice to destroying the family bonds and innocent lives that she began the play by defending.

Even outside the disruption of traditional values that characterized the period when the play was performed and thus made its central issues compelling, Hecuba's action is characterized by the ambiguity of female action in general. Women in ancient Greece did play an important role in religious ritual and in lamenting the dead and wielded considerable power in the domestic sphere. Yet physically, Greek women were popularly considered too weak, irrational, credulous, and unstable for constructive action.[14] Female persuasion, especially by elite women, was thought able to threaten a man's reason.[15] Greek doctors argued that, unless women were pregnant or menstruating, their wombs might wander around their bodies, causing mental or physical illness. Ideally, respectable women should stay at home as much as possible, avoid gossip or any threat to their reputation, maintain silence in public, and let men act for them. In tragedy, by contrast, revenge can grow out of traditional female lamentation and sense of obligation to the dead, as it still does in cultures where vendetta is the only or primary mode of justice.[16] In this context, the grief of helpless women like Hecuba becomes not only pitiable, but potentially dangerous. Moreover in myth women like the Lemnian women or the Egyptian Danaids later cited in the play by Hecuba have an uncanny ability to act in unity, a wordless communication perhaps learned from years of being culturally silenced, but also from sharing in festal dancing, worshiping the gods, and lamenting the dead. The 1966 film *The Battle of Algiers*, where the veiled women of Algiers started carrying around bombs under their robes and acting as guerrillas, could serve as a comparably disconcerting modern example of violent female collective action.

In the contemporary world, it is important for the reader of *Hecuba* to modify Hamlet's question: what's Hecuba to **us** or **we** to Hecuba that **we** should weep for her? Why has this rarely produced play suddenly begun to receive a number of important professional performances in recent years? Proper burial remains a significant moral and social issue in the world today. In the wake of the military dictatorships in Argentina and other Latin American countries, for example, grief for the many 'disappeared' persons remains unassuaged to the present. The destruction of the World Trade Center in 9/11 generated heated arguments over what was to happen to the remains of the bodies that the site held. In *Hecuba*, the fact that both the gods and the Greeks unite to assure the burial of the former queen's children serves to highlight Polymestor's outrageous neglect of burial ritual in the case of Polydorus.

The issues in the play that arise out of the treatment of prisoners or a conquered enemy are relevant to contemporary debates about the potential violations by the US of international laws of war in their torture of prisoners at Guantanamo, the killing of civilians to destroy American enemies in drone attacks, or the challenge to the authority of other nations in order to defend human rights or oppose genocide. How does our world deal with those who, like Hecuba, no longer have any real access to human rights or justice, and explode in anguish over its loss? Equally important, whichever position we take, *how* we talk about the questions central to *Hecuba* (as well as to Thucydides) bears a critical relation to what we do. And in many respects, as this book will demonstrate, the arguments that the beleaguered and always rational (if impassioned) Hecuba poses in this play to those in power in defense of the powerless are perhaps even more central to its meaning than Hecuba's shocking reversal from victim to successful avenger.

2

Theatrical Festivals and the Mythical Tradition

The Performance Context

Although central and articulate female characters like Hecuba appear in nearly every Greek tragedy, the performance of tragedy was entirely male dominated. Athenian plays were performed in large outdoor theaters. The theater festival at the City Dionysia where *Hecuba* was first presented was the most important annual event in Athens. The size of the audience at this date ranged according to current estimates from around 5,000 to over 15,000.[1] Male citizens of Athens were the primary audience, and tickets may even at this early period have been subsidized for those citizens who could not afford them. Because the plays were performed when the seas were readily passable in the month Elaphebolion (late March), Athens' allies in the Delian League during the Peloponnesian Wars came to the festival, displayed their annual tribute in the theater, and attended the plays along with foreigners and fans from other Greek cities. Children and some slaves could attend, and women may or may not have been included, at least in small numbers—the issue is still hotly debated.[2] The three actors who performed all the roles in each play along with additional mute figures were male citizens; a male *aulos* or double pipe player (often not a citizen) accompanied the chorus. Every Athenian male citizen would have grown up dancing and singing at the City Dionysia in tragic and comic choruses as well as in *dithyrambic* choruses of fifty men or fifty boys from the ten tribes of Athens performed at the same festival. The opening phases of the festival included a large public procession and sacrifices to the god Dionysus in whose honor the plays were performed; libations were offered in the theater by the ten generals of the *polis* (city-state), state benefactors received gold crowns for their generosity and loyalty, war orphans reaching their majority marched with armor donated by the city; seats at the front of the theater were reserved for important officials and other figures.[3]

Male citizens in the theater audience also served in the military and on juries and attended political assemblies in the Attic democracy. Their direct experience in public life made Athenian citizens in the audience aficionados of the kind of long speeches about justice and politics central to this play as well as of the musical, dance, and lyrical traditions central to tragic performance. Tragedy tried to deal through mythical stories with central political and social issues for a democratic audience who had the power to act on them in the future. At the same time, since tragedy drew plots from Panhellenic myths and became increasingly popular outside Athens as the fifth century wore on, foreign visitors could have been equally engaged in productions from their own perspectives.

The theater of Dionysus was located on the south-east slope of the Acropolis. The *orchêstra*, a large circular, rectangular, or trapezoidal dancing floor (the shape remains controversial for the fifth-century theater)[4] surrounded on three sides by the audience seated in wooden bleachers was occupied by the fifteen person chorus, who performed choral songs and were witnesses to the action from their entrance, rarely leaving the stage before the end of the play. Actors could enter, like the chorus, from the two wings (*eisodoi* or *parodoi*) to the right and left of the orchestra and share the orchestra with the chorus, but also entered from the central door of a temporary wooden stage building or *skênê* erected for each festival that may or may not have had a low stage before it. In *Hecuba*, one wing led in the audience's imagination to the Greek camp, Achilles' tomb, and, beyond it, Polymestor's dwelling. The other probably led to the seashore and may have been used by the maidservant who went to fetch water for Polymestor's body, and Polymestor's ghost if he entered stage level.

Hecuba, her daughter, her servant, and her other silent female supporters come in and out of the stage building imagined in this play to be a tent probably reserved for new slaves of the Greek general Agamemnon.[5] The *skênê* becomes the heroine's de facto 'house' for most of the play.[6] The challenging role of Hecuba was played by the *protagonist* or first actor; the second actor would have played Polyxena and Polymestor, both difficult singing parts, as well as Talthybius and Hecuba's maid servant; the third actor probably took the part of Polydorus and the Greek generals Odysseus and Agamemnon (Demosthenes 18.267 says that the orator Aeschines did a poor job as third actor with the role of Polydorus).[7] As in many tragedies, the female-dominated space in the *skênê* proves dangerous to their male enemy, in this case, Polymestor. He emerges from the *skênê* at the end of the play blinded and on all fours, perhaps accompanied by his slaughtered children on a platform (the *ekkyklêma*) often brought out to display dead bodies on the tragic stage. Since the chorus also consists of recently enslaved Trojan women who have taken a risk to inform their former queen of events in the Greek camp, the play brings a group of women outside of spaces in which they traditionally belonged to react eloquently to a series of male visitors from the Greek army and finally from Thrace itself. From the moment of the choral entrance the stage is thus dominated by the presence of female characters.[8] The ghost of Polydorus, whose entry will be discussed below, might have opened the play from a position on top of the stage building, entering from a wing, or, less probably, using the *mêchanê* or machine usually occupied by divinities.

Each playwright and his wealthy producer or *chorêgos* presented three tragedies and one satyr play (a burlesque of Greek myth with a chorus of satyrs or horse men) in competition with plays by two other playwrights for a prize. We do not know what plays were produced with *Hecuba* or how it fared in the contest, although the controversial but popular Euripides rarely received first prize (four times in his life, one posthumously). Some scholars have argued that Euripides' extant satyr play *Cyclops* was presented with *Hecuba*, since the play involved Odysseus' blinding and humiliating of the giant ogre of the *Odyssey*; metrical evidence suggests, however, that *Cyclops* was performed later than 424 BCE, the most likely date for *Hecuba*.[9]

The Mythical Tradition

Euripides, the youngest of the three canonical tragic playwrights of the fifth century, was born sometime between 485–80 BCE and died in 406 in Macedonia; he wrote more than ninety plays, of which eighteen survive (*Rhesus*, attributed to Euripides, is generally thought to be by a fourth-century author). He presented his first play in 455 BCE, and *Bacchae* and *Iphigenia in Aulis* were performed in 405 BCE after his death. In the following centuries his plays eclipsed those of his famous predecessors Aeschylus and Sophocles in re-performances on stages throughout the Mediterranean world. Every Greek playwright modified and re-imagined both theatrical performance and Greek mythical tradition, but Euripides seems to have been especially prone to radical innovations. The first part of *Hecuba* modifies traditions probably familiar to the audience from earlier Greek epic and lyric, but the story of Polymestor's murder of Polydorus and his subsequent blinding by Hecuba and her women were, as noted earlier, probably an entirely new and a shocking development for the audience, especially since in his prologue speech the ghost of Polydorus does not predict this turn of events.

Each playwright's version of the myth made his play more innovative and exciting in the tragic competition. The Trojan Queen

Hecuba stood out as a figure subjected to extraordinary suffering from Homer onwards and Euripides has preserved and intensified this aspect of the character. In the *Iliad*, both she and King Priam lose many sons to the Trojan War, but the death of Hecuba's son Hector, chief defender of Troy, receives the greatest attention. In *Iliad* Book 6, Hecuba attempts to delay Hector's return to the battlefield with maternal solicitude before accompanying a group of women to Athena's temple to propitiate the goddess. Shortly before Hector is about to meet his death in his fatal duel with Achilles, she pleads with her son to return to the safety of the city as she stands on the walls and exposes her maternal breast in a moving speech (22.79–89). In Book 24, she offers one of three poignant laments at Hector's funeral along with his wife Andromache and Helen (24.747–60). The slightly later post-Iliadic lost epic cycle poems that dwelt on the fall of Troy included the hideous death of Priam, as well as Hecuba's enslavement to the Greeks and the death of more children and grandchildren.

In Euripides' own later play *Trojan Women* (415 BCE) Cassandra leaves Hecuba to become concubine to Agamemnon, her daughter Polyxena is sacrificed on the tomb of Achilles, Hector's son Astyanax is torn from the arms of his mother Andromache and thrown from the walls of Troy and buried by the Trojan women; the fallen city of Troy itself begins to burn in the concluding scene as the queen descends into lonely half-mad despair while the remaining Trojan women depart for a slavery in Greece already repeatedly anticipated in Homer. Euripides' earlier play *Hecuba* also makes a point of intensifying these extraordinary losses familiar from earlier tradition and giving Hecuba the central role. Here we are told she gave Priam fifty children, rather than the fourteen mentioned in the *Iliad*, and in the course of the play she loses all those remaining alive except Cassandra, who will soon, as Polymestor prophesies, die in Argos. (Her son the prophet Helenus in some versions survived in Molossia, but here Hecuba knows nothing of his fate).[10] When Agamemnon hears from Hecuba of the death of her last son Polydorus, he remarks, 'Alas, alas, what woman was born to such misfortune.' Hecuba replies 'None exists, unless you speak of Tychê (Fortune) herself.' (785–6).[11] The chorus also stresses this same point (659–60 and 721–2).

Since the post-Homeric epic cycle and other archaic lyric also treated Polyxena's death or sacrifice, her fate would not have come as a surprise to Euripides' audience. In the sixth-century BCE epic *Sack of Troy* (*Iliupersis*) she was killed by Achilles' son Neoptolemus at Achilles' tomb after the sack of Troy (see also Ibycus, fragment 307 PMG/PMGF) and the *Cypria* (scholion to *Hecuba* 41, F27 Davies) had her wounded by Diomedes and Odysseus and buried by Neoptolemus. Achilles' ghost made an appearance in the early epic *Nostoi* (*Returns Home*) where he tried to prevent the departure of the Greeks with dire prophecies; Achilles' sacrifice of twelve Trojans at Patroclus' funeral in the *Iliad* (21, 23, 26–9, 175–6) had already established his inclination to demand excessive sacrifices. The archaic sixth–fifth-century BCE lyric poet Simonides (fragment 557 PMG) and Sophocles' lost play *Polyxena* very likely anticipated Euripides in sacrificing Polyxena to Achilles' ghost (Longinus, *On the Sublime* 15.7), although we are uncertain of the date of Sophocles' play.[12] It seems probable, however, that Euripides further moralized and politicized or even invented the debate over her death.[13]

Polygnotus' 'Sack of Troy' painted on the northern wing of the Propylaea on the Athenian acropolis c. 432 BCE reportedly showed Polyxena about to be slaughtered next to Achilles' tomb (Pausanias, *Description of Greece* 1.22.6).[14] Two important pre-Euripidean archaic visual images show Polyxena apparently sacrificed against her will like Iphigenia in Aeschylus' *Agamemnon*. A black-figure Tyrrhenian amphora by the Timiades Painter of around 550 BCE (British Museum, London 1897.7-27.2) shows a group of warriors (Amphilochus, Antiphates, and Ajax son of Oileus, the hero who tried to rape Cassandra at the altar of Athena) holding Polyxena, heavily bound in her robe or *peplos* over a flaming altar as blood drips from her neck. (**Figure 1 and cover**) Neoptolemus seizes her hair while stabbing her neck with his sword. The scene is framed by the aged warrior Nestor

Figure 1. The Sacrifice of Polyxena, Tyrrhenian black-figure amphora by the Timiades Painter dated c. 550 BCE (British Museum, London 1897.7–27.2).

and Diomedes on the left and Achilles' tutor Phoenix turning his head away in apparent dissent on the right.

A late archaic marble sarcophagus at the Çanakkale Museum in Turkey dated to 520–500 BCE and discovered in a location near Troy and the original tomb of Achilles shows the same scene on its north side (**Figure 2**).[15] Three men hold a resisting Polyxena, wearing a thin *chitôn* (robe) that reveals her vulnerable body, in front of the egg-shaped tomb of Achilles and a tripod to the right. Neoptolemus seizes Polyxena's hair and cuts her throat as if she were a sacrificial animal. His direct gaze into Polyxena's eyes appears suggestively erotic.[16] To the left stands a female figure with a walking stick who is pinching her nose (perhaps an aged servant)[17] and six mourning women wearing loose chitons in different poses. The scene spills over to the west side of the sarcophagus where a veiled Hecuba, her aged face marked by crow's feet, sits holding a staff surrounded by a leafless tree and two additional mourners (perhaps Cassandra and Andromache). On the east side (not shown), a veiled woman shares a couch and converses with a younger woman with whom she entwines her feet. She is attended by three women, two holding a pitcher and wine strainer, a pyxis (cosmetics box), and an egg, and one embracing the back of the veiled woman. A mysterious scene on the south side seems to mix funerary and festive themes.[18] A veiled woman seated on a throne with legs that look like a winged Eros or Love holds a flower in one hand, an egg in the other. Six female attendants on either side bring a mirror, a fillet, a lyre, a fan, two alabastra (vases), and a plate of eggs. On the right is a female piper, a female cithara (lyre) player, a chorus of four pyrrhic dancers (dancers in armor), a female dancer with castanets, and three more female onlookers, one clutching her garment. The frieze as a whole puts civilized (and perhaps funerary) domestic scenes in counterpoint to a scene of violence and suffering inflicted by men on women in the outside world. This much discussed and controversial continuous frieze locates Polyxena's and Hecuba's

Figure 2, A and B. Drawings based on an original by Nurten Sevinç of the sacrifice of Polyxena on two sides of a late archaic marble sarcophagus at the Çanakkale Archaeological Museum in Turkey dated c. 520–500 BCE. The circles represent small drill holes. Courtesy of the Troy Excavation Project.

story in a world filled with women who lament, attend, and even serve as a musical chorus to events depicted on the sarcophagus in a fashion later appropriated in different ways by tragic versions of this story.[19] In Euripides' play a mourning Hecuba does sit veiled after her daughter's in-this-case voluntary sacrifice surrounded by a chorus of Trojan women who share her grief. This chorus repeatedly evokes in their odes peaceful scenes involving women sharing domestic life before the fall of Troy or ritual scenes in which they hope to participate in the future.

Another fragmentary archaic cup attributed to Hieron and Macron dated around 500 BCE shows a sword-bearing Neoptolemus leading Polyxena to Achilles' grave mound as she leans back in fear (Paris, Louvre G 153). In a black-figure hydria by the Leagros group in the Staatliche Museum, Berlin (F1902), also dated around 500 BCE, Polyxena is led by Neoptolemus to a mound with a chthonic snake coiled around it and a ghostly warrior above it. Finally, in a Clazomenian sarcophagus from the late sixth-century BCE (Leiden 1.1896/12.1), Neoptolemus leads Polyxena to Achilles' tomb holding her wrist in a gesture often used by a bridegroom leading his bride.[20]

Versions of the story that invented a symbolic 'marriage' or romance between Achilles and Polyxena are probably post-Euripidean.[21] Nevertheless, Euripides apparently intended Polyxena's sacrifice in Thrace to echo the story of Iphigenia's sacrifice by her father Agamemnon at the beginning of the Trojan War at Aulis.[22] The play confronts the Greeks with a second decision to kill an innocent virgin to ensure their voyage.[23] The language used to describe Achilles' demand for a female prize in *Hecuba* also recalls Agamemnon's quarrel with Achilles over a female prize (*geras*) in *Iliad* 1 and builds on the angry Achilles' concern with his fame throughout much of the epic.[24] Even more important, Polyxena's eloquent voluntary acceptance of her sacrifice is almost certainly and characteristically (given the poet's fondness for heroic sacrificial youths) invented by Euripides. Euripides' play thus gives both Polyxena and Hecuba a more active role than tradition allowed them. Their activism became canonical in many later versions.

Euripides also introduces innovations in the case of some of the male characters. In the *Iliad* (22.48) Polydorus, in this case a son of Priam and Laothoe (not Hecuba), is quickly dispatched by Achilles when the great hero returns to battle (*Iliad* 20.407–18, 21.91,

22.46–48); although Priam had as in Euripides hoped to keep his youngest and especially dear son out of combat, he had not dispatched him with gold to Thrace.[25] The figure of Polymestor and the events occurring in the Thracian setting for this play might possibly reflect a local Thracian myth. Yet the devious Polymestor's lack of any named ancestry and his name, which means 'much-planning,' suggest that he was invented for his role in this play. In other Greek poetry Achilles' tomb is generally represented as near Troy at Sigeum, not across the Hellespont in the harsh but fertile sea coast of the Thracian Chersonese; nor does he otherwise refuse to allow the Greek fleet to proceed without honor to his tomb. There is also no known precedent for the Thracian father of Hecuba in this play. In the *Iliad* her father is Dymas, not Cisseus.[26] Finally, the Agamemnon of this play in many respects resembles his Iliadic character, but Odysseus more closely resembles the sophistic Odysseus of much later Greek tragedy.[27]

Hecuba's novel revenge on Polymestor perhaps develops from the queen's appetite for savage grief that appears at *Iliad* 24.212–13 in her desire to eat Achilles' liver raw due to his mistreatment of Hector's dead body. Yet in earlier tradition her story, as far as we know, did not end, as in Euripides, with a transformation into a dog and a tomb on a promontory of the Hellespont called Cynossema, 'Bitch's Tomb.' We hear nothing of her end in the extant epic cycle. In *Trojan Women* she is assigned as a slave to Odysseus but probably, as Cassandra predicts, died in Troy (*Trojan Women*, 427) rather than leaving with Agamemnon. Other sources have her rescued by the god Apollo and brought to Lycia (Stesichorus fragment 198 PMG and Pausanias, *Description of Greece* 10.27.2) or jumping off Odysseus' ship to her death.[28]

By setting the play in Thrace Euripides established in the story of the Greeks' return from Troy a novel, liminal, barbarian-dominated space between fallen Troy and Greece.[29] In other plays that Euripides writes shortly after this one, such as *Iphigenia Among the Taurians* and

Helen, Euripides also locates Greek characters in newly imagined barbarian settings. These foreign settings allow developing a complex contrast between conceptions of 'Greek' and 'barbarian.' The Thracians of this play are described as armed horsemen, but otherwise we learn little from the play about Polymestor's kingdom beyond the presence of the prophetic cult of the half-wild god Dionysus. The name of Hecuba's new Thracian father Cisseus, 'man of ivy,' also suggests a connection to Dionysus. The setting may have capitalized on the ambivalent relation of Euripides' audience to Thrace at this time. Parts of Thrace, which controlled access to the fertile grain-producing lands of the Black Sea, were colonized by Athenians in the sixth century BCE and taken back from Persia at end of the second Persian War (480–479 BCE). In the period of the Peloponnesian War the local Odrysian monarchy had an 'equivocal attitude to the interests of both Sparta and Athens in Thrace' and had abandoned the Athenian cause in favor of the Spartans prior to the fall of Amphipolis in 424 BCE.[30] The play represents Polymestor as a questionable and greedy ally to both Greeks and Trojans. Thucydides notes the avarice and murderous violence of the Odrysian kings (2.97, 7.29.4) and Thracians were proverbially thought unreliable: 'Thracians do not understand oaths' (Zenobius 4.32). The fact that Attic slaves often came from Thrace could have colored the audience's response to Polymestor as a generic Thracian in Euripides' play.[31]

The overall effect of these innovations in *Hecuba* is to sandwich a novel revenge plot within a more familiar mythological framework. Later Euripidean revenge plays create even more extravagant and unfamiliar deviations from the mythical tradition. In *Orestes*, for example, Pylades, Orestes, and Electra attempt and fail to kill Helen and then take her daughter Hermione hostage since they cannot escape their own condemnation for the killing of Clytemnestra. It takes the appearance of the god Apollo on the machine to bring this wildly veering plot back to a relatively familiar conclusion. In *Hecuba*, as in *Orestes*, the heroine both constructs and carries out her own novel plot, but in this case the play concludes with the prophecy that Polymestor received from Dionysus rather than a divine intervention.

3

Dramatic Structure and Unity

The Action of the Play

Prologue and lyric scenes: the ghost of Polydorus; Hecuba and Polyxena (1–215)

The ghost of Polydorus opens the play by explaining why Polymestor murdered his previously well-tended guest for gold after the fall of Troy and announces that the gods have promised his burial before the day is out. He predicts his sister Polyxena's sacrifice and pities his mother. Yet he does not, as for example the goddess Aphrodite does at the start of Euripides' *Hippolytus*, anticipate the revenge plot that dominates the second half of the play.[1]

After her son's ghost departs, the grieving Hecuba awakens from a prophetic and frightening nightmare; the audience might have expected that she would then receive the terrible news of her dead son. Instead, Hecuba almost immediately learns from a chorus of Trojan women that her daughter Polyxena is to be sacrificed to Achilles' ghost (*parodos*, 98–151); her troubles never seem to stop. She calls Polyxena from within and laments with her daughter.

First Episode: Hecuba, Odysseus, and Polyxena (216–443)

When the Greek hero, Odysseus, who had persuaded the army to demand Polyxena's sacrifice, arrives to take the girl away, Hecuba tries to resist by making a passionate and articulate claim on him. She argues that she once saved his life when he came into Troy in disguise to spy out the territory. Odysseus owes her a life in return. If he chooses to, he could persuade the army to change its mind about Polyxena's sacrifice. She argues that the Greeks now unjustly sacrifice innocent women whom they had made an effort to spare during the fall of Troy according to the standards common in war. Why should Polyxena be sacrificed instead of the guilty Helen of Troy, or even Hecuba herself?

But the demagogic Odysseus' lack of sympathy for an appeal that Hecuba has made as one civilized aristocrat and individual to another is reflected in his legalistic response to her religious appeal, as she formally supplicates him by clasping his knees with her arms. Of course, Odysseus says, he is willing to return Hecuba's favor by sparing *her* life, but not her daughter's. For if the hero Achilles, who died for Greece, is not honored as soldiers should be, army discipline and motivation will disappear. The public interest must take precedence over individual debts, such as his to Hecuba. Everyone, he adds, Greeks and Trojans alike, have suffered in this war, and fine distinctions over individual suffering are irrelevant. Despite her mother's strong resistance, Hecuba's daughter Polyxena then chooses heroically to go to her death voluntarily rather than attempt to cling to a humiliating life of slavery. (*The first choral stasimon follows at 444-83*).

Second Episode: Talthybius and Hecuba (484-628)

After her daughter leaves for death, Hecuba is soon moved by the Greek herald Talthybius' account of Polyxena's noble last moments and the admiration her behavior evoked from the army. Hecuba's aristocratic values that she tried to use to persuade Odysseus have been attacked, but at least her daughter has died incarnating traditional courage and nobility. (*The second choral stasimon follows at 629-57*).

Third Episode: Serving Woman, Hecuba, and Agamemnon (658-904)

Then Hecuba learns the truth about her murdered son Polydorus, her last hope, from her maidservant who has gone to fetch water for Polyxena's burial on the beach. Something shatters in her. A kind of madness begins to take over as she bursts into song: 'I am utterly destroyed, I no longer live. O child, child, aiai, I begin a wild bacchic song, having just now learned of these evils from a spirit of vengeance' (683-87).[2] 'Unspeakable, unnameable, beyond amazement, unholy, and unendurable. Where is justice among allies/guest friends?' (*xenoi*, 714-15).[3] Once again, Hecuba tries to appeal for justice to the Greeks, this time to the expedition's leader, Agamemnon. She invokes moral standards that must be respected if civilization is to be preserved. This time Agamemnon, partly due to his love for his Trojan mistress Cassandra, pities Hecuba and agrees that Polymestor deserves punishment. But, although a barbarian, the vicious Polymestor is a Greek ally, and once again, the army's interests must, in Agamemnon's view, take precedence over a crime committed against an enemy. Besides, Agamemnon adds, he does not want to look as if he is motivated, as he was in the earlier debate over Polyxena, by his Trojan mistress Cassandra.

Hecuba now recognizes that even the powerful have no real freedom to pursue a virtuous or just course. She says to Agamemnon, 'There is no man who is free; either he is slave to money or to chance, or the city-masses or written law prevent him from following his bent as he decides. Since you are afraid, then, and cede the mob the upper hand, I shall free you of this fear myself. Give me your complicity if I plan some harm against my son's killer, but do not share the deed'

(864–71). Hecuba feels forced to turn to herself and the other Trojan women for justice. Agamemnon agrees he will back her if she, as he thinks unlikely for a woman, succeeds in her revenge. (*The third choral stasimon follows at 905–52*).

Fourth Episode: Polymestor and Hecuba (953–1022)

Hecuba sends for Polymestor and his sons and then puts on a tremendous act for them, shamelessly exploiting a traditional femininity to which she has no intention of adhering. She lures her three victims into the women's tent by promising the greedy and lying Polymestor secrets about more hidden Trojan gold. (*A brief lyrical intervention by the chorus occurs at 1024–34*).

Exodos (last episode): Polymestor, Hecuba, and Agamemnon (1035–1295)

The women disarm Polymestor, separate him from his children, and then descend on their victims en masse. The blinded Polymestor summons Agamemnon, who stages a 'trial' between Polymestor and Hecuba. Polymestor pretends he killed Polydorus in the interests of himself and his allies the Greeks. He is humiliated to be destroyed by a woman and wants the Greeks to share his horror. But Hecuba has learned her lesson from her previous failures to persuade the Greek leaders, and now at least partially adopts a rhetoric and form of expedient argument she learned from them. She gives Agamemnon a way out of his alliance with Polymestor by demonstrating not as she originally argued that Polymestor was unjust to *her*, but that he has betrayed his alliance with the Greeks and will make them look bad if they defend his greed and misbehavior.

  She wins the debate, but the play has further consolidated a moral universe where no clear standards prevail and more violence and instability are promised for the future. Civilized principles have given way to military power and expediency, and few of the Greeks will survive to profit from their victory over Troy. Polymestor predicts that Agamemnon and Cassandra will die at the hands of his wife Clytemnestra, Hecuba will mount the mast of Agamemnon's ship, become a dog with fiery eyes, and plunge into the sea; her grave will serve as a beacon for sailors. The original audience also knew that Agamemnon's own death would be avenged by his son Orestes and that many of the enslaved Trojan women of the play's chorus would die at sea with their masters on the return journey that they leave to undertake at the conclusion of the play.

The 'Problem of Unity'

As we have seen, *Hecuba* contains several major episodes, and Euripides appears to have been the first author to combine them into one play. The first part of the play deals with the sacrifice of Polyxena and the second begins with Hecuba's discovery of the body of Polydorus and ends with her effort to avenge his death. This second part concludes with the 'trial' scene in which Agamemnon presides as judge and a departure of all the characters for the futures partly predicted by Polymestor. Critics struggling to interpret the play have disagreed about whether the play lacks unity due to the very different tone and result of these central episodes.

The critical reception of the play has from the Renaissance on been highly influenced by Aristotle's *Poetics*, which praises tragedies based on a unified action or *praxis* where all episodes contribute to an organic whole evolving in a chain of necessary and probable events. Aristotle's central example, Sophocles' *Oedipus Tyrannos*, is unified by the hero's search for the killer of Laius/his own identity. The plot of *Hecuba* in the view of many modern critics lacks this kind of easily identifiable action. Polydorus in the prologue of *Hecuba* predicts both the sacrifice of his sister and his own eventual burial. The play from this perspective has a certain physical symmetry. It closes as Hecuba departs to bury her two children. Polydorus' covered body probably remains on stage until it is carried off in this final scene.[4] Polymestor's two visible dead children now match Hecuba's own recent losses. Hecuba's presence on stage throughout most of the play and her evolving reactions to its central events provide a continuous focus.[5] Nevertheless, the prologue, as noted earlier, does not predict Hecuba's effort to take revenge, an event which was probably also without precedent in the mythological tradition. Hence the play in this respect deliberately lacks the obvious momentum and seeming inevitability of a play like *Oedipus Tyrannos* even if it evolves as a series of causally related events.

The abrupt transitions in the play have led critics to look elsewhere to explain its structure, and especially to give it a thematic coherence. For a significant number of critics, the play traces an evolution in the character of Hecuba brought on by her increasingly catastrophic losses. Hecuba begins the play as a figure that relies on traditional aristocratic ethics, sometimes defined in the play as a product of *nomos* or unwritten law and tradition that universally governs both divine and human reality. She seeks survival and then justice for her children and supports the bonds of guest friendship (*xenia*) and the need to bury the dead. Yet Hecuba is now a slave, and her ability to enforce such ethics is highly limited. She must attempt to persuade those in power who do not share her pain and seem to feel at least initially invulnerable to it.[6] In the view of some of these critics, Hecuba increasingly relies on potentially dubious modes of persuasion linked with contemporary Athenian rhetoric and sophistic argument.[7] Many argue that the play traces her gradual moral corruption in a world that is also corrupt and demoralized, as she turns to self-help justice that relies on deception, abuses the principles of hospitality by doing violence to her guest Polymestor,[8] and punishes not only the guilty Polymestor, but his innocent children. Her transformation into a dog from this perspective affirms this interpretation; Hecuba has already figuratively become the bestial figure into which she evolves. In order to achieve her revenge, she also becomes humiliatingly indifferent to her status as a slave, a status that her daughter Polyxena prefers to die rather than accept.[9]

In a modified view of this position, James Kastely argued that Euripides 'places a protagonist skilled in rhetoric in a situation in which those in power, insulated from the pain of others, cannot be reached through persuasion ... Euripides raises questions about rhetoric not to impugn it, however, but to develop a complex and sophisticated justification for it ... It would not be an exaggeration to say that the play's protagonist is as much rhetoric as it is Hecuba, for the ethical integrity of rhetoric is as much at stake as the ethical identity of Hecuba.'[10] In the debased and relentlessly episodic world of the play, where leaders are enslaved to power, 'a claim of justice is inevitably translated into a need for revenge, as the willingness to take revenge becomes an act of resistance and an assertion of dignity. In the pursuit of revenge, Hecuba refuses to accept the right of the powerful to disregard the humanity of those without power.'[11] Although Kastely also takes the position that the now brutalized Hecuba becomes 'incapable of integration into a society' and reveals both her own blindness to the pain of others and a numbness to her own future, her rhetoric retains a 'continuous articulation of *nomos* (law).'[12] 'For Hecuba, rhetoric is not a cynical strategy adapted when appeals to *nomos* fail; rather, the practice embodies the aspiration of those who would be free and just.'[13] Similarly, Judith Mossman argues that 'words, their use and abuse, rhetoric and persuasion, are of desperate importance to the poet in this play, as in many others,' even if 'they are useless in the face of physical violence or simple expediency.'[14] In short, from this perspective the play demonstrates the need for effective rhetoric that relies on stable principles in precarious historical situations as an alternative to violence.

Despite her failure to persuade Odysseus, Agamemnon, and finally Polymestor of her views, other critics more strongly defend the necessity of Hecuba's choice to take action, the consistency of her character, and, like Kastely, the authority of her speech. Hecuba's commitment to justice and her principled resistance not only to those in power, but even to her own daughter's attempt to interpret her sacrifice as an act of noble freedom defines her throughout.[15] Moreover, she, as Richard Buxton puts it, 'never ceases to try to put her will into action.'[16] Hecuba turns to self-help justice only after failing to persuade Agamemnon to act for her.[17] In Athens, 'it was the duty of the family of a murdered person [including women where no men remain] to obtain retribution for the injury he had suffered.'[18] By such traditional standards she could not leave her son unavenged. In Greek myth the anger of unavenged victims can even pollute whole cities, as did the murder of Laius in *Oedipus Tyrannos*.[19] Hecuba, Agamemnon, and even the blinded Polymestor describe her revenge (*timôria*, 749, 756, 882, 1258; 790, 843) as *dikê* (punishment or justice, 844, 1052–3, 1253);[20] critics must therefore be careful not to impose anachronistic views on the play.[21] This includes the symmetrical killing of Polymestor's children (discussed further below), which deprives the king of heirs just as he did Priam and Hecuba. In enacting revenge Hecuba attempts to carry out violent justice in a world that from her perspective accepts sacrificing her innocent daughter to Achilles and puts the views of the democratic assembly and a relation of *philia* (friendship or allegiance) to the barbarian Polymestor above the civilized principles that she constantly evokes, principles on which Greek ethics traditionally relied. Although Hecuba's views can rely on seemingly outmoded traditional aristocratic perspectives and reflect a distrust of a democratic collective, her arguments in pursuit of justice also include democratic dimensions, especially the principle of equality under the law, at all stages. 'Powerful men should have no power over things they ought not, nor when they are prosperous think they will always do well ... You Greeks have a law about bloodshed; it is the same for free men and for slaves alike' (282–3). Some critics have also noted that although males have been the initial instigators of offenses against Hecuba and her children, the play, as is often the case in Greek tragedy, conveniently transfers the enactment of violence to women.[22] Unquestionably, all of the deaths and punishments in this play remain terrible and excessive, as do the imminent deaths of both Hecuba and Agamemnon. Yet from this second perspective, Hecuba's forthcoming brief transformation into a dog, an animal that could also be linked with fertility, maternity, loyalty, and guardianship, prefigures the heroic function of her tomb, which serves as a beacon to preserve the lives of sailors.[23]

These different general interpretations of the action are not easily mediated, especially since they continue to overlap in many details. My discussion will attempt to enrich our understanding of the play by looking in much more detail at the sequence of scenes and arguments without relying on a particular case for 'unity' or thematic coherence in advance. Only then can we attempt to revisit the controversies developed in the play's interpretation and reception from the Renaissance, which viewed the play quite differently, to the present. It is also important to remember that this play was designed from its inception for performance, and that stage action can produce reactions in an audience that may not be consistent with the analysis of the words spoken alone. Aristotle argued that character on the tragic stage is defined solely by action and choice (*Poetics* 1450b, 8–10); the beleaguered Hecuba never ceases trying to make things happen. Attempts to create a psychologically coherent persona for Hecuba must confront Greek tragedy's lack of interest in exploring the inner selves of its central figures[24] and an acting style that relied on modulation of voice and gesture by figures wearing masks and costumes that largely covered their bodies.

Regardless of the views of members of an audience toward revenge, the play arguably produces active sympathy for Hecuba's successful revenge against the patently villainous Polymestor as it evolves, despite the shocking final scene. The breathless rapidity of the action,[25] with the exception of a central pause for contemplating the sacrifice of Polyxena, exerts a powerful dramatic force as well. Physical embraces, whether between mother and daughter or between suppliant and supplicated, constantly frame the action. Bodies speak in this play.[26] The blinded Polymestor crawls on the stage and tries to seize his torturers. Talthybius vividly describes the death of Polyxena, as she rips open her robe and reveals a beautiful body resembling a statue. Hecuba urgently wants her aged body to speak to those whom she wishes to persuade. Similarly, characters repeatedly invite the intense gaze of others, asking for pity or other responses from those in power; the dog that Hecuba becomes retains her fiery eyes. During one choral ode, a Trojan woman gazes at herself in a mirror the night before the fall of Troy (925).[27] The choral odes, which can bear a tangential relation to the stage events, regularly intervene in the action, re-contextualize it, and allow the audience to step back from the relentless pace of the play. They also open our perspective toward past and future. Finally, the reaction of the original audience as well as later audiences to this play is inevitably conditioned by the politics of the world in which it is performed. For the original audience, the politics of war and empire stand behind the representation of the relations between the powerful and the powerless in this play and the words that struggle to express the play's contradictions.[28]

4

Interpreting the Action: Hecuba and the Power of Persuasion

Ghosts in Greek Tragedy

Renaissance revenge tragedies typically began with a ghost who sought revenge for unjust murder. The pitifully slaughtered Polydorus seeks only lament and burial from his mother, and assures the audience that he will receive it before the day is out. Ghostly appearances can generate revenge in Greek tragedy; the dead Clytemnestra does so just after the opening of Aeschylus' *Eumenides*, as she stirs her Erinyes or Furies to awake and continue their pursuit of her son Orestes for matricide.[1] The ghost of the Persian king Darius is summoned and appears to advise his wife in Aeschylus' *Persians*, but Agamemnon, whose ghost is summoned by his children and the chorus of slave women in Aeschylus' *Libation Bearers* to support Orestes' revenge for his father, does not. Achilles, whose ghostly appearance and demand for a *geras* (prize of honor) is reported in Polydorus' speech, may have already appeared on stage in Sophocles' *Polyxena*. One Greek vase apparently shows a chorus of six identically dressed soldiers (half of a twelve-person tragic chorus) dancing before a tomb from which a bearded ghost that they may have invoked has apparently emerged (Attic red-figure column krater, c. 490 BCE, Basel BS 415). Nevertheless, few ghosts appear in the extant texts of Greek tragedy, so a ghostly appearance probably still had the power of novelty. Perhaps the parody of Polydorus' opening lines in Aristophanes' *Gerytades* (fragment 156,1-2 K-A) indicates that he interpreted this ghost as yet another exciting Euripidean surprise.

If Polydorus' ghost appears above the action as he hovers above his mother (30-1), either on the roof of the *skênê* or (as seems less likely given his language) even on the machine generally reserved in tragedy for divinities, his position gives him a more than human authority despite his youthful pathos. His pity for his mother over her coming losses of himself and Polyxena invites a response to her suffering that is soon pointedly resisted by the Greek leader Odysseus. If Polydorus is on stage level (as his wish to move out of Hecuba's way, *ekpodôn*, in line 52 might suggest), his presence more easily merges with the nightmares that haunt the terrified Hecuba at her entrance.[2] In either case, the opening establishes a strong perspective of sympathy for Hecuba.

As is typical of Euripides' prologues, Polydorus also introduces the audience not only to the poet's choice of mythological events to explore but to a Thracian context that was unlikely to be familiar. His name, Polydorus, 'giver of many gifts' or 'given many gifts,' perhaps links him with the figure of Hades below, who can be ironically described with similar epithets;[3] both his name and that of his sister Polyxena ('entertaining many guests') also resonate with the theme of guest friendship and hospitality central to the play.[4] Polydorus interprets Hecuba's fall into slavery and misery as an attempt by an unknown god to counterbalance her former prosperity (57-8). This view opens up a question to which others return in later scenes. At the same time, most of the action of this play, aside from the intervention of Achilles' ghost, seems to be generated by humans, and if gods play a role, we can only see traces of their presence in the promise of burial to Polydorus or, more controversially, in the final return of the wind (discussed below) that enables the Greeks' departure at the close of the play.

Hecuba's Entrance

Hecuba's entrance, supported by several silent women, reinforces the pity generated by her son. Bursting into song, she tries in vain to reject her frightening dream of a hind torn from her lap by a wolf's bloody jaws (90–1). The image characterizes in advance Achilles' ghost as bestially violent (perhaps the image could apply as well to Polydorus and Polymestor). Song in Greek tragedy always represents an important higher register for a Greek actor, but mourning Trojan women like Hecuba, Cassandra, and Andromache seem almost preprogrammed to sing in Euripides.[5] Hecuba fears, if disputed sections of the text are sound, for both her son and her daughter. She is aware that Achilles has demanded a *geras* (prize) from among the women of Troy.[6] Her hopes that Polyxena will evade this fate are immediately crushed by the hasty appearance of the chorus of captive Trojan slave women, who report that the Greek assembly has decided to sacrifice Polyxena and that Odysseus will soon arrive to claim her. Their representation of the democratic Greek assembly strongly colors the audience's preparation for Odysseus' appearance. Achilles in his golden armor appeared above his tomb and demanded honor. Agamemnon, due to his relation to Cassandra, argued against a sacrificial victim for the tomb. Two Athenian sons of the Attic hero Theseus argue for the sacrifice and against Agamemnon's sympathy to Cassandra. Finally Odysseus, described by the chorus as a shifty, smooth talking, demagogic speaker, persuaded the divided assembly that they should not dishonor the 'best of the Achaeans' in order to avoid sacrificing slaves.[7] This anachronistic depiction of a democratic rather than epic-style assembly clearly invites the audience to interpret it in anachronistic terms. Moreover, although Achilles' demand would seem to require a favorable response since the fleet cannot sail without propitiating him, the choral description suggests that the assembly viewed itself as having a genuine choice to make on this occasion.⁸ It thus invites the audience to reconsider the assembly's decision.

Distraught, Hecuba calls Polyxena from her tent. Hecuba's sung lament at 154–76 is soon matched by Polyxena from 197–215. Yet Polyxena's pity for her mother rather than for her own fate instead reinforces the sympathetic response to Hecuba's suffering generated by Polydorus' ghost.⁹ The chorus urges Hecuba to pray to the gods above and below at altars and temples and supplicate them for help. If such altars and temples are available in Thrace,¹⁰ Hecuba has in any case no time to do so, but as proves to be characteristic of the queen, she will, despite Odysseus' entering request for her immediate acquiescence to power, attempt verbal and physical persuasion of her oppressors instead.

The Debate between Odysseus and Hecuba

Hecuba self-consciously describes the scene with Odysseus as a great *agôn* (229, the standard word for a dramatic debate or contest).¹¹ Critics have frequently remarked on her rational rhetorical eloquence.¹² She consistently sizes up her audience. Her use of an ordered structure, balanced antitheses, rhetorical questions, and appeals to emotion are present in her speeches from the start; moreover, Judith Mossman rightly argues that her speeches are more exciting than those of other characters.¹³ She begins by pleading for free speech as a slave. This plea (full of lament and without tears, 230) will also rely above all on generating pity, an emotional response that Hecuba's world has up to now generously given her in the play. She will physically reinforce this plea by touching Odysseus' cheek and embracing his knees. The important ritual act of supplication is rarely rejected on the tragic stage.¹⁴

Hecuba wishes to bring Odysseus to her side by making him a *philos* or friend, who owes her kindness/reciprocity (*charis*), rather than an enemy. Hence she opens with a short dialog reminding Odysseus of an event otherwise unknown in the epic tradition and probably invented by Euripides. In the *Odyssey*, we hear that Odysseus once came into Troy as a spy in beggar's disguise (4, 244–56). Helen recognized and spared him. In Hecuba's new version, Helen revealed the secret to Hecuba and Odysseus was forced to supplicate the queen and accept the structural position of the slave that Hecuba now is. Hecuba spared Odysseus and he admits she saved his life. In this story, Hecuba crossed the friend–enemy boundary and respected suppliancy. Her act implies a sense of shared ethical, cultural, and personal ground between Greeks and Trojans that she now wishes to exploit.

Hecuba then contrasts Odysseus' demagogic public relation to the assembly with his current mistreatment of a friend, Hecuba. Here she relies on a respected Greek tradition of doing good to friends and bad only to enemies. She reinforces her disrespect for the masses and their vulnerability to clever specious argument (*sophisma*, 258) by pointing out that human rather than animal sacrifice at a tomb is in principle unfitting (the term *prepei*, 261, 'it is fitting', makes her point more vulnerable, since it does not directly rely on moral tradition); Achilles is not justified in demanding the death of an innocent enemy; an equally beautiful and more appropriate victim would be Helen, who did harm Achilles.[15] These points sum up what she calls an argument based on justice (*tôi dikaiôi*, 271).

Now Hecuba turns to pity—a request to step back and recognize common humanity. She supplicates Odysseus, reminding him that Polyxena is all she has left; she is her city, nurse, staff, and guide (281). Supplication must by implication be respected and in principle protected by the gods because human life is vulnerable. If the army spared the Trojan women whom they dragged from altars during the fall of Troy, Hecuba asserts, they should not disrespect that choice now. Greek law (*nomos*) protects both slave and free (291), hence Greek public standards support in principle her private plea. If, as she knows from the chorus, Odysseus persuaded the army to make the choice to sacrifice Polyxena before, his authority (if not necessarily his argument) can persuade the army to spare Polyxena now. The chorus reinforces Hecuba's plea by interpreting it as something that could not fail to generate the pity at which she clearly aimed (296–8).

Both Hecuba's argument and her gestures aim at creating a personal bond with Odysseus that relies on traditional aristocratic ethics, but she also attempts to reinforce her position with more general political points about the status of slave and free (e.g., Attic law that mandates protection of slaves) and the injustice of human sacrifice, an act which tragedy consistently treats as a corruption of proper religious ritual unless it is voluntary and for a positive cause such as insuring victory in war. She tries to rely, as she will in her next large speech, on both *charis* (a sense of reciprocity) and *dikê* (justice).

Odysseus interprets Hecuba's speech as a dangerous expression of anger that could alienate a person who speaks best/for the best. As is generally the case in tragedy, if not in reality or on the Homeric battlefield, Odysseus recognizes her suppliancy, but on narrow terms. He will spare her life. But he stands by his earlier argument to the assembly. Achilles, a friend to the army, takes precedence because he died for Greece, and only barbarians would invoke claims to personal friendship over honoring dead soldiers. Here the verb he chooses echoes and challenges her use of the term *nomos*, law or tradition (*nomitomen*, 326). He argues that cities cannot muster armies if they do not respect the honor of their soldiers. Odysseus too would want the lasting honor of and access to a tomb. (Here he perhaps echoes Odysseus' lines from Sophocles' *Ajax* 1365–7, where he argues for burying Ajax; if so he now uses the argument to reject rather than reinforce pity). For this honor is 'a favor (*charis*) which lasts' (320). Moreover, he adds, Hecuba's plea for pity must be put in perspective. Greek old men, women and young brides have suffered equally from the Trojan War and must endure, as Hecuba now should.

Odysseus de facto wins the argument, although both sides raise compelling issues. Yet as commentators have remarked, Odysseus' argument is anachronistic. Achilles did not in the *Iliad* fight for Greece, but for the honor of himself and his Myrmidons. Odysseus ignores/is oblivious to both Hecuba's case against human sacrifice in this context and her own situation, which is considerably worse, given her loss of city and family and her enslavement, than that of those in Greece who have lost relatives in the war; nor does he have any evidence that barbarians, as he asserts (328–31), unlike the Greeks, fail to honor their dead.[16] Hecuba did not request life; in her argument Polyxena is the equivalent of her life, and her own life is not in fact in jeopardy,[17] although she has little interest in living. The democratic army was far more uncertain than Odysseus that Polyxena should be sacrificed. Despite his powerful argument on this point, Odysseus is arguably loyal to maintaining the strength of the army, but not to examining unjust injuries it can inflict.[18] The Attic democracy, especially after Pericles, did honor those who died for the city, and put its collective needs above those of the individual; Odysseus' position reflects that view.[19]

Hecuba's eloquent arguments, her emphasis if by no means entire focus on individual suffering and bonds that traditionally govern individual more than civic relations by implication belong to a pre-city state world (or to an early stage of Athenian democracy).[20] The chorus realistically interprets Hecuba's failure to persuade Odysseus here as due to her condition; it is the lot of slaves to endure violence and wrong perpetrated by those in power (331–2). Her view of *dikê* (justice) and *charis* (reciprocity) stands no chance due to inequality of speakers and the views that they represent in this debate.[21] (See Thucydides 5.84–11 mentioned earlier.) For the original audience, then, Odysseus' argument, despite its omissions, speaks to political reality. Hecuba, however, while recognizing the failure of her speech, can only turn once again towards trying to generate pity, as she urges

Polyxena herself to supplicate Odysseus because he himself has children.

Polyxena's Sacrifice

Euripides was particularly attracted to the theme of voluntary sacrifice of a young virginal figure, more often female than male, for the benefit of family, city, or nation (that is, Panhellenic ventures). A young daughter of Heracles sacrificed her life for the family of Heracles in Euripides' earlier play *Children of Heracles*, and after *Hecuba*, Creon's young son Menoeceus sacrifices himself to save Thebes in his later *Phoenician Women*; the daughters of Erectheus in *Erectheus* and Iphigenia in *Iphigenia in Aulis* also choose to accept sacrifice for the *polis* (city-state) or Greece respectively. In *Hecuba*'s novel version, Polyxena refuses to resist her sacrifice, but has no interest in the cause of appeasing or honoring Achilles' ghost. Polyxena rejects her mother's request to supplicate Odysseus, who is in any case withdrawing from her to avoid being supplicated (342–4). Instead, she prefers to die freely and courageously on her own terms.

Polyxena, once a princess for whose hand the most powerful princes competed, has no wish to accept a life of slavery involving humble domestic tasks and perhaps being forced to accept another bought-slave as a partner.[22] Hecuba and the chorus recognize the nobility of Polyxena's stance, but Hecuba immediately requests to die in her place or with her daughter. Odysseus, almost verging on pity, thinks one death enough (389–90). Polyxena has no wish to see her mother publically humiliated by violence and she begins a moving farewell to her resisting mother, ironically reminding her of the supposed survival of Cassandra and Polydorus. Embracing her mother's breast and almost surrendering to lament, she departs with veiled head leaving her mother to collapse with outstretched hands that continue to resist her daughter's departure. This farewell scene includes no sung exchange between mother and daughter, perhaps a sign of Hecuba's refusal to accept Polyxena's choice and Polyxena's effort at self-control.[23] Hecuba ends the scene lying prone and covered in despair.

Following the first choral *stasimon* or inter-episodic song to be discussed later, the Greek messenger Talthybius arrives to summon Hecuba for her daughter's burial. Talthybius, who in contrast to Odysseus pities Hecuba and weeps a second time for Polyxena, reports on Polyxena's remarkable death that has stirred the army to nobility and essentially offers for her a funeral encomium.

Neoptolemus, the son of Achilles, he tells her, began the ceremony with a prayer to his father asking for an immediate and safe return. He prepared his sword for slaughter and readied men to hold down the girl as in the vase paintings noted earlier (see **Figures 1 and 2**). Polyxena asks to die freely. She strips her gown to the waist, revealing a body resembling a Greek statue, and invites a blow to breast or neck. Neoptolemus cuts her throat, and she falls modestly, without revealing the parts of her body that should not be exposed to male eyes. The army responds to her bravery, throwing leaves on her corpse and preparing a funeral pyre. They urge each other to find ornaments to honor the girl. Hecuba, eager to lament and bury her daughter and still stung by her loss, sends her serving woman for water to bathe the body and goes to seek ornaments for her burial. She fears necrophilia on the part of the army (604–8).[24] Polyxena's courage slightly assuages her grief, as she meditates, in a fashion popular in mid-fifth century philosophy, on whether nature or nurture can explain such remarkable nobility.[25]

This scene has produced divergent responses from critics.[26] The army apparently responds to Polyxena's gesture as heroic; leaves were traditionally thrown on the body of men who were victorious in athletic games.[27] Polyxena's offer of her breast or neck to Neoptolemus' weapon remains puzzling. Sacrificial victims were generally killed by slicing the neck; warriors might be struck in the chest, but they did not offer themselves to the blow.[28] Although Iphigenia may have shed her robes in the description of her sacrifice in Aeschylus' *Agamemnon* (the text at 231–47 is hard to interpret) and is also compared to a work of art, Euripides' other sacrificial victims remain covered and previous visual representations of Polyxena's death discussed earlier do the same. The Çanakkale sarcophagus does reveal her body beneath her thin *chitôn*, however, and a later (end of the fourth century BCE) sarcophagus in Orvieto in the Museo dell'Opera de del Duomo, Torre San Severo shows Achilles standing at his tomb and watching a nude Polyxena slaughtered by Neoptolemus.[29] Nevertheless, archaic Greek art generally limits the nudity of respectable women either to extreme moments of vulnerability to violence, such as Cassandra taking refuge at Athena's altar during the fall of Troy or the dying daughters of Niobe, although a few vases depict a nude bride preparing a nuptial bath.[30] Although deceased virgins are often described as 'brides of Hades' in Greek literature, this motif remains largely repressed here. A slight hint may appear in the gesture undertaken by Neoptolemus as he leads Polyxena to the altar with his hand on her wrist; this gesture was a standard part of a wedding ceremony; Polyxena is also described by Hecuba as a calf, bride no bride, a maiden, no maiden at 612. This suggests she has become a symbolic bride of Achilles in Hades.

What, then, can explain Polyxena's choice to theatricalize her death and invite the desiring gaze of the army? Some critics have been repelled by this apparent objectification, while others view it as a remarkable display of pathos, heroism, and freedom. Nancy Rabinowitz notes contradictions between Polyxena's apparent winning of male honor, her resistance to victimage, and her assertion of subjectivity and her complicity in her own objectification as an object of desire. In reality, females have in her view no access to 'heroism' except as self-sacrifice. Her death assures the perpetuation of bankrupt values and simply 'allows power to rest comfortably in its own power.'[31] Judith Mossman argues that the scene aims to produce pathos not a sexual response, whereas Ruth Scodel thinks that her gesture restores Polyxena to her previous status as a valuable object of beauty and desire to men of her own class and, while potentially inviting physical abuse (a possibility that Hecuba fears), she wins for herself honor, burial, and gifts.[32] At the very least, Polyxena's gesture, by speaking through the body as well as words, underlines the power of performing her choice rather than simply articulating it. On the other hand, her choice for a noble death is not possible for others in the play and her sacrifice does not even facilitate an immediate departure for the fleet.[33] Hecuba now leaves the stage to fetch trinkets for Polyxena's burial, and the second action of the play begins.[34]

Hecuba's Supplication to Agamemnon

After the brief respite provided to Hecuba in the Talthybius scene and a choral ode, Hecuba's servant returns with the covered and mutilated body of Polydorus, which she has found on the seashore while fetching water for Polyxena's burial. Hecuba at first believes the body to be that of Polyxena or Cassandra, but soon discovers the terrible truth. She bursts into excited song (the *dochmiac* meter she uses here is reserved in tragedy for moments of high excitement) and begins what she calls a bacchic song, having learned of her new evils from a spirit of revenge or *alastôr*. She instantly recognizes, very likely from the terrible dream that she now recalls, that the perpetrator is Polymestor, who is motivated by gold. From this first moment, then, we know Hecuba feels compelled to seek justice for this unspeakable crime and betrayal. Yet although possessed with a spirit of vengeance, her speech never loses coherence or rationality.

Before Hecuba has fully absorbed this new grief, Agamemnon arrives to find out why Hecuba has not arrived to bury her daughter.

Hecuba debates at some length to herself about whether to appeal to Agamemnon for help.[35] She fears another rejection of the kind she received from Odysseus, then wonders if she is over-interpreting Agamemnon's hostility. Finally, since she knows she cannot avenge her children without him (749–50), she decides to supplicate the king. The plural that she uses here of the children she wishes to avenge may not be significant (it can be grammatically identified as a generalizing plural), but it is possible that she psychologically wants to avenge both children, not just Polydorus, by killing the two sons of Polymestor.[36] Agamemnon mistakenly thinks she is supplicating him for freedom, which he is willing to grant, but Hecuba asserts that she will tolerate slavery for the rest of her life if she can achieve revenge (756–67). While this last remark has been viewed as degrading, it could also stress a fierce priority for justice in a person who has already repeatedly emphasized that she has lost anything worth living for.[37] As she explains the story of Polydorus, Agamemnon himself instantly recognizes Polymestor's motive (gold) and expresses sympathy for Hecuba's plight. Hecuba's long and eloquent speech that follows is both an expanded appeal for pity and a more general and powerful case for justice.[38]

Hecuba asks Agamemnon to avenge Polymestor's violation of *xenia* (guest friendship), sacred rites (*hosia*) and *nomos* (law, tradition, or convention). She then famously adds: 'Though we [probably meaning we humans] are [probably metaphorically] slaves and perhaps powerless, the gods are powerful along with the law (*nomos*) that rules them. Through/by reason of *nomos* we believe in gods and live distinguishing justice and injustice. If this law is referred to you and is corrupted, and those who kill guest friends or dare to plunder what is sacred to the gods pay no penalty, nothing is safe/equal (*sôs* or *isôs*, the text is uncertain here) in the affairs of men' (798–805). Others translate *nomos* here as tradition or convention, and argue that the passage takes a sophistic perspective that asserts that humans invent *nomos* and the gods that enforce them in order to insure the authority of such conventions.³⁹ The sophist Critias argues, for example, that 'a wise man invented the gods to deter men from evil' (TrGF 43F). I agree with those interpreters who believe that Hecuba here argues that a higher law governs the universe/nature itself, including gods (who even in Homer are not entirely omnipotent) and men, and makes justice possible and a moral order intelligible.⁴⁰ Any purely conventional *nomos* would lack the authority that she is trying to rely on here.⁴¹ The existence of this law affirms human belief in divinities; its violation destroys stability or equality (depending on the text) in the human world. A fragment of the poet Pindar brings civilizing violence into the purview of this *nomos*. '*Nomos*, the king of all, of mortals and immortals, guides them as it justifies the utmost violence with a sovereign hand. I bring as witness the deeds of Heracles …' (fragment 169 Snell).⁴² In asking Agamemnon to consider Polymestor's actions shameful, she urges him to contemplate her own case and to take pity, as if looking at a picture, on a queen turned slave, old, alone, childless, and without a city. He is a leader (*tyrannos*), and as a slave she, by normal Greek standards, must rely on Agamemnon.

In response to this appeal, Agamemnon apparently attempts to remove himself (specifically his foot, *ekpodôn*) from Hecuba's extended suppliant embrace.⁴³ Her argument on broader terms has seemingly failed, and she now wishes for herself and all others not the greater knowledge that ideally ought to be pursued, but more effective persuasive speech (rhetoric), even at the cost of paying to acquire it, as those in Athens did with sophists at the time of this play rather than in the epic world of the dramatic setting (814–19).⁴⁴ This suggests that she views her previous appeal to *nomos* as something more than the mode of persuasion (*peithô*) that she will now adopt, a mode of persuasion that is in actuality sovereign (*tyrannos*, 816) over men. Her next move has scandalized many critics.⁴⁵ Again contemplating her powerlessness (no children, a burning city, slavery) she turns to a point perhaps alien to (*xenon*, 824) or unavailing for (*kenon*, again the text is uncertain) her argument, the erotic appeal of her daughter the prophetess Cassandra, Agamemnon's new concubine. She argues that Agamemnon owes Cassandra and her family *charis* (gratitude) for those nights of love.[46] Polydorus is by this logic Agamemnon's de facto brother-in-law. Hecuba then invents a second extraordinary physical image to reinforce her plea, which may appear inspired by the living statue that Polyxena became at the moment of her sacrifice. She wishes her arms, hands, hair, and feet had voices created through divine or mortal craft to supplicate Agamemnon and offer eloquent pleas. In other words, she wishes that she could become a miraculous living statue, a body that can speak its anguish and make words effective, like those designed by the mythical inventor and artist Daedalus who created living automata. Echoing the tradition that adjures doing good to friends and bad to enemies, she asserts finally that 'it is a good/noble man's duty to serve justice (*dikê*) and treat bad men badly everywhere'(844–5).

The chorus interprets this speech as an attempt to make enemies into friends and friends into foes, a boundary crossing that Hecuba had already attempted with Odysseus as well as Agamemnon in this play, but, as we shall see, goes on to deny in her last speech. Agamemnon, unlike Odysseus, responds to her appeal for pity if not her plea for *philia* (relationship by 'marriage'). (In fact most Greeks in the play do feel pity.) For the sake of the gods, he would like Polymestor to pay for his unholiness. But the army considers Polymestor *philios* (friendly, an ally) and Agamemnon cannot appear to act for Cassandra when Polymestor, not Polydorus, is their ally. He is only willing to help if he can avoid political censure. By not stipulating how Hecuba will carry out her revenge, however, he becomes in principle complicit with it. He also reduces justice to 'convenience,' since his assent depends on the inability of the army to sail due to lack of wind.[47]

We know of an earlier historical incident in which Athenians let barbarians take revenge on their enemies and kill children.[48] In a story told by the Greek historian Herodotus (*Histories* 7, 33; 9, 116–120), a Persian named Artayctes got hold of a treasure of a man named Protesilaus in Thrace and desecrated a shrine of the gods. After the Athenians defeated the Persians in their famous war against them, they took Artayctes prisoner. The people of the Elaeus in the Chersonese wanted to exact revenge on behalf of Protesilaus. The Athenian commander, Xanthippus, the father of the famous Athenian statesman Pericles, let them nail Artayctes to a plank and stone his son to death before his eyes. Like Xanthippus, Agamemnon lets barbarian women, rather than Greeks, take a bloody revenge on Polymestor. Euripides may have been thinking of this incident when he refuses to have his male leaders enact Hecuba's mode of justice; Greeks rarely used crucifixion or blinding as punishments, and blinding in tragedy, such as the self-blinding of Oedipus in *Oedipus Tyrannos*, is viewed with horror.[49] Yet in myths about the aftermath of the Trojan War and during the Peloponnesian War Greeks inflicted many cruel, unjust punishments on their enemies. Perhaps the play conveniently attributes to barbarian women a ferocity all too familiar and tolerated among Greeks.[50]

A *scholion* on a similar passage in Sophocles' *Ajax* (520) expressed outrage over Hecuba's 'pandering' of her daughter, and many later critics have interpreted this turn to an appeal based on sexual desire (*erôs*) as shameful.[51] (A scholion at *Hecuba* 825, however, defends Hecuba against the charge of 'prostituting' her daughter.) In epic, however, the bond between female captive and master can evolve through sexual *charis* (reciprocity, sexual favor) into something like a marital bond.[52] Achilles envisions his captive Briseis as the emotional equivalent of a wife, and his friend Patroclus had made Briseis hope that she might one day become one. Agamemnon prefers his concubine Chryseis to his wife Clytemnestra in *Iliad* 1, and has in this play chosen Cassandra as his prize. Cassandra in Euripides' *Trojan Women* even calls her relation to Agamemnon a 'marriage', though with considerable irony. Historically, even in classical Athens concubines could be treated like wives, who also became loyal to their husbands through the sexual bond, although their children were bastards and not legal heirs to their fathers. A law cited in the oration *Against Eratosthenes* by Lysias treats rape of a concubine kept to produce children as equivalent to that of a wife. Despite the *Ajax* scholion, modern critics have not treated as outrageous the slave concubine Tecmessa's appeal to the *charis* (sexual favor) that Ajax had received from her as his partner when she tries to make the case for his survival (*Ajax*, 514–19) and Ajax treats her bastard son as his heir. Hecuba knows from the chorus that Agamemnon had earlier argued against sacrificing Polyxena for Cassandra's sake. Archaic friendship involved an exchange of favors of many kinds. Because Hecuba now appeals to Agamemnon's personal relation to her, her appeal is foreign to and less powerful than her 'universal' claim for *nomos*. Yet that universal argument has apparently failed, and she now hopes, as did Tecmessa, to make Agamemnon feel emotionally vulnerable by the only route left to her. This second appeal also fails to make Agamemnon act for her, however, because it is precisely the relation to Cassandra that makes Agamemnon vulnerable to the army.[53] Hecuba, in contrast to her rhetorical 'contest' with Odysseus, did attempt in the first part of the scene to make the kind of generalizing appeal that Odysseus uses to counter her own speech. Moreover, the desperate turn once again to using an argument based on her personal relation to a Greek leader does at least open the door to taking justice into her own hands.

5

Hecuba's Revenge

Hecuba now concludes to Agamemnon that no man is free; all, including the powerful, are slaves to money, to chance, to the mob or to written law (which was thought to ensure equality in Athens' democracy).[1] In this play a leader who knows justice claims he cannot act, yet recognizing universal 'slavery' can liberate a powerless woman to act freely just as the humiliation of slavery did Polyxena.[2] With sudden authority, Hecuba claims she will 'free' Agamemnon of fear of the mob that governs him and asks for complicity and covert support if she, not he, takes action. Agamemnon is shocked. How will she, a helpless old woman, take action? By sword or poison (the latter a 'female' weapon)? On whom could she rely? Hecuba will rely on a different mob, a crowd of women in the tents who can master men through mass action and cunning and deprive them of male heirs, like the Egyptian Danaids, who with one exception killed their unwanted husbands on their wedding night, or the Lemnian women, who killed all men on the island of Lemnos except their queen's father for scorning them.[3] Hecuba instructs Agamemnon to give her serving woman safe passage through the army to bring Polymestor and his sons to her tent and to delay a joint funeral for her children until she has accomplished her goal. Since the wind currently prevents the Greeks from sailing, Agamemnon agrees to this request and echoes Hecuba's concluding point that the bad should suffer and the good succeed. He has apparently accepted her argument up to this point.[4]

Yet like the Attic king Aegeus in Euripides' *Medea* or the Attic king Demophon in Euripides' *Children of Heracles*, he will leave Hecuba to enact revenge herself. Aegeus promised to protect Medea in Athens, but she had to find her way there herself (he does not know the details of her revenge plan) and Demophon allowed Heracles' mother Alcmene to punish her captured persecutor Eurystheus.

Hecuba now moves to enact her revenge. Her scene with Polymestor reflects a change in tone and strategy, as she relies on cunning (previously she is entirely forthright) to achieve her goals. At his entrance Polymestor immediately establishes his villainy and invites the audience to enjoy, at least for a time, his forthcoming comeuppance.[5] He clearly had not been on his way to see Hecuba when he encountered her maid servant as he claimed; nor was he likely to have been away earlier. His hypocrisy is affirmed by his pompous sententious remarks on the fragility of human fortune and the inefficacy of lament. His outright lies—he claims that Polydorus is alive and eager to see his mother—contrast with the vivid reality of Polydorus' covered corpse that he mistakes for that of Polyxena. (I agree with those who think Polydorus' corpse remains on stage until the end of the play when it is carried off for burial.)[6] Hecuba disarms Polymestor by pretending to believe these lies, by luring his mute attendants to leave the stage, by playing on his greed to learn further secret sources of Trojan treasure, and by assuring him of the entirely female population in the tents. Even her refusal to look at him, which she pretends is due to her loss of status and her feminine modesty, conceals the expression of eyes that the audience knows are burning for revenge (968–75).

The chorus clearly expects Polymestor to be killed in the tent (1024–34). Instead, his sons are killed and he is blinded in a scene that apparently echoes moments in the death of Agamemnon in Aeschylus' *Oresteia*.[7] Agamemnon's offstage death cry in *Agamemnon* had perhaps become standard in such scenes. But when the chorus heroically considers bursting in to help, as did the chorus in

Agamemnon, and when Hecuba emerges like Clytemnestra to claim justice (*dikên didonai*, 1052–3) and announces the display of the bodies of the children and the imminent appearance of the blinded king, her act perhaps suggests the provocative scene of the earlier play more extensively.[8] What comes next, however, is quite different from the Aeschylean scene. Polymestor, who is not dead, enters singing, largely in the excited dochmiac meter, and crawling on all fours like the beast he has for the moment become. He wishes to tear apart and eat his avengers in response to an act that he characterizes as Dionysiac. The women are in his words 'Bacchants of Hades' (1076, and later 'murderous dogs,' 1173) about to throw their prey without burial into the wilds. His perhaps exaggerated description here may recall Hecuba's earlier reference to the avenging bacchic song (also sung in the dochmiac meter) that will drive her to revenge and remind the audience of more extreme Dionysiac myths in which maddened women collectively punish those who reject the god, such as king Pentheus in Euripides' later *Bacchae*, using their bare hands.[9] (At 1183–4, however, the chorus of women objects to his generalizations blaming women as a 'race'.) Like the mythical Orion (1101), who was once blinded and cured by the sun god Helios, Polymestor calls for help and begs for a cure for his eyes.[10] Others have suggested ways in which the scene might recall the blinding of the ogre Cyclops in *Odyssey* Book 9, which also appears in Euripides' own probably later satyr play, *Cyclops*.[11] An Apulian lourophoros of about 340–325 BCE by the Darius Painter (London, British Museum 1900.5-19.1) was probably inspired by a revival of Euripides' play and shows a blinded Polymestor groping after Hecuba.

Adult males, especially in Euripides, rarely sing in Greek tragedy; barbarians, starting from Xerxes in Aeschylus' *Persians*, can do so. This burst into violent, emotional song potentially undermines the normal identity of mature male characters (the blinded Oedipus also sings in Sophocles' *Oedipus Tyrannus*), but in this case Polymestor's language also sets him apart from a rational male. As Christopher Collard described his entrance: 'His crippling pain is conveyed by theatrical entry on all fours ... and a changed mask all bloody ... Irregular shrieks of agony and despair; cries of hate; broken, illogically ordered thought, mostly phrased as imploring questions; staccato delivery (the *monody* has no connective particles between clauses whatsoever); frantically repetitious and redundant language; wild imaginings; extreme metrical unevenness—all portray bewildered rage.'[12] As he notes, Polymestor's desperate questions echo those in Hecuba's despairing opening monody over her losses at 162–4.[13]

The Final 'Trial'

The revenge action culminates in a formal debate adjudicated by Agamemnon. The audience, however, knows that Agamemnon pretends ignorance about what might have happened and is orchestrating this event. It is a primitive version of a 'trial' or arbitration with a jury of one staged before a few silent Greek attendants and many women. Agamemnon no longer plays the role of the friend/ally from whom Polymestor hopes for aid, but of a Greek curbing an uncivilized barbarian's rage. Polymestor is already punished for his crime, so the only real issue here is how the two speakers will defend their perspectives on the event. Nevertheless, I agree with those critics who argue that although Agamemnon permitted Hecuba to enact her revenge, he did not promise a specific response to her undertaking, and even if the audience knows that Hecuba for the first time occupies the standard winning second position in tragic debate, it cannot predict why Agamemnon chooses to stage the debate and what he as judge will say.[14] In this debate, the emotional figure who needs justice and demands pity is now the prosecutor Polymestor. Both his savagery and his confirmed lies compromise his claim to have killed Polydorus for strictly political reasons that he thinks Agamemnon would find persuasive. Most of Polymestor's rhetorically unsophisticated speech evolves as a vivid messenger speech describing his punishment that he expects will be persuasive in its case against women and slaves and produce pathos.[15] Although Polymestor claims his murder did a favor (*charis*, 1175) for the Greeks by eliminating an enemy, his motive for killing Polydorus also supposedly represents his own self-interest in avoiding future attacks on Thrace by a surviving son of Priam that might bring the Greeks back to Troy. Yet the audience's curiosity has perhaps been whetted more for his report of the gory crime than his justification for it. How did a group of women achieve their goal? In his description the women's impressive unity and strategy partially balances the horror of their acts in the sense that they have become a community acting collectively to achieve justice.

Hecuba's Trial Speech

We know from the extensive remains of ancient court speeches that evoking pity could be part of a standard defense speech (as in Polymestor's speech). Yet Hecuba's speech has for the first time no recourse to personal appeals for sympathy and pity. Here Hecuba plays the part of coolly logical defendant; her arguments aim at justice, far less than expediency.[16] Tragic figures in Euripides often lament that words and deeds do not have a transparent relation to each other. Hecuba begins by asserting that 'men ought never to have a tongue more powerful than their deeds' (1187–8). She aims to challenge the truth of Polymestor's claims, but she now does so in terms that could invite contemporary fears about deceptively persuasive public rhetoric.[17] Her argument is marked by more self-conscious rhetorical stages than her earlier speeches, including a preamble (1195) that launches the above formulaic attack on rhetoric that applies better to her own speech—at least in terms of its rhetorical skill—than Polymestor's. Her first point relies on the rhetorical technique of *eikos* or probability.[18] Polymestor's claim that he killed Polydorus for the Greeks is, she argues, impossible. Logically, as Odysseus had earlier suggested, barbarians and Greeks cannot be friends.[19] (Critics have noted here that the Greeks in fact treated Polymestor as an ally.)[20] Polymestor was not a relative or seeking to become one so he cannot be defined as friend from a personal perspective.[21] Here her use of hypophora, a rhetorical device laying aside an objection imagined to be raised by an opponent, disguises the fact the Polymestor did not directly make claims on this basis.[22] At the same time Hecuba has to demonstrate to Agamemnon that Polymestor no longer deserves to be an ally (*philios*), as Agamemnon called him, and so must insist on Polymestor's personal motive for serving Greek interests before denying that he is doing so.[23] Moreover, the Greeks would not have returned to Troy to ravage his crops for protecting Polydorus as he claimed. No, Hecuba now asserts, the motive was gold, a factor that Polymestor had pointedly failed to mention and explain in his own speech. As an ally, she now argues using a rhetorical device known as a hypothetical syllogism,[24] Polymestor should either have killed the boy or brought him to the Greeks earlier and shared the gold when they needed it. Killing Polydorus after the fall of Troy makes clear that his motive was greed. By contrast, standing by the principles of guest friendship (still by implication possible among barbarians) would on the one hand have brought Polymestor true reputation and prosperity. Agamemnon, whom as her master she claims to have no wish to rebuke, will on the other hand, she concludes, gain a bad repute for supporting a man unholy and unjust to his friends.

Hecuba has here reasserted once again an argument for justice and traditional *nomos*; Polymestor has violated guest friendship and burial ritual and should not be rewarded for his bad acts. Her emphasis on motive again resonates, as does her public rhetorical style, with practice in Attic court cases.[25] Yet she also tries once again to force Agamemnon to respect what she interprets as universal principles in his role as leader. Although she herself had attempted to establish and exploit a relation of *philia* with both Odysseus and Agamemnon, she now must argue for and perhaps correctly recognizes the impossibility in her world of such *philia* between barbarians and Greeks.[26] At the same time, she does not resolve the conflicts that the play has revealed between *philia* to the army and among individuals. This last speech retains Hecuba's consistent reliance throughout the play on persuasive speech; she has not abandoned *nomos* for *peithô*, though her style of persuasion now suits a public context and no longer relies on her vulnerability and beleaguered maternal and former aristocratic status. Critics rightly perceive a move to a narrower strategy here; her argument sounds different because it emphasizes exposing Polymestor's misrepresentation of his public relation as ally to the Greeks. She entirely ignores the horrific details of the punishment she and her women surprisingly succeeded in enacting. Instead she aims for the moment and perhaps, if only in speech, to bring private and public justice together. This speech allows her in its closing lines to win a victory for her own conception of justice and to offer an implicit self-defense of her revenge.[27]

The play thus finally, regardless of her revenge, gives Hecuba political and perhaps even divine support. The chorus for the first time praises Hecuba's argument (1238–9). Agamemnon affirms its public effectiveness by endorsing it point by point (1240–51) and criticizes Polymestor's. He agrees that Polymestor killed Polydorus for greed and not for the sake of Agamemnon and the Greeks. Killing guests is revolting to Greeks (as opposed to barbarians) and Agamemnon would be censured for exonerating such an act. Polymestor must endure the consequences of his action. Agamemnon then announces that the windlessness that kept the fleet from departing has now stopped. Is this a sign from the gods?[28] Does it rise now because Polymestor's impiety has been punished?[29]

After this 'trial' Polymestor remains anguished above all about being humiliated by women and slaves. Hecuba reasserts the justice of her act and rejoices in the revenge. Polymestor admits that he received *dikê* (justice or punishment, 1253). Since her women not Hecuba physically exacted justice for her (1160–71), her revenge conforms to spirit of Attic law that did not allow an injured party to punish a criminal directly.[30] The choice of blinding rather than murder remains an open question that the play itself has raised, but the pattern of symmetrical imposition of suffering appears elsewhere in earlier tragedy. Greek tragic heroines like Antigone or Phaedra explicitly wish that the men who have challenged or injured them will experience suffering like their own. (Sophocles *Antigone* 925–8, Euripides *Hippolytus* 729–31; Medea is similarly motivated in her last scene with Jason). The plays fulfill these wishes. Hecuba, though she does not explicitly say so, seems to have wished Polymestor to experience the loss of children, including the mutilation of a child's body, that she suffered from him. But, since blindness and prophecy are linked in tragedy (the blind prophet Teiresias, the blind Oedipus in Sophocles' *Oedipus Tyrannos*) perhaps the blinding also prepares for Polymestor's sudden shift to announcing prophecies that he heard from Dionysus. Hecuba, he asserts, will not continue to rejoice. She will climb the ship's masthead, fall from it and drown, and become a bitch with flaming eyes.[31] Her tomb, named Cynossema or bitch's grave, will become a beacon for sailors. Hecuba responds that she does not care since she has completed her revenge. But Agamemnon will not tolerate Polymestor's next prophecy in which he claims that Clytemnestra will kill both Cassandra and himself with a bloody axe in Argos.[32] He gags and dispatches him to deserted islands before turning to organizing departure for all. Hecuba will bury her children and the chorus of women must prepare to meet their hard future by exiting to tents and then harbors.

Many critics see Polymestor's prophecy as affirming a deserved punishment for both Hecuba and Agamemnon, and expressing the queen's moral corruption, because she will lose her power of human speech and become the beast that bloody revenge and the sacrifice of innocent children has made of both herself and Polymestor.[33] Others, however, and especially Anne Burnett, analyze this metamorphosis differently.[34] Burnett argues that 'Euripides does not ask his audience to repudiate Hecuba's revenge as an inadmissible atrocity. Polymestor has been presented throughout as a greedy and grotesque barbarian, a savage who feeds on others' civility, and in these final scenes his punishment is displayed as an ugly but exact communal response to his savagery. Within the community this accurate retaliation is preliminary to the *nomos* of burial, and it is followed in the natural world by a revival of favoring winds.'[35] From this critical perspective, Hecuba no longer cares for life now that her justice is complete and her children are dead. Dogs can also embody fertility, fiercely protective maternity, and faithful guardianship of human borders and habitations.[36] Hecuba will apparently drown almost immediately, and her transformation may have allowed Euripides to link her death to a known landmark that protected sailors during their treacherous voyage on the Hellespont.[37] Ovid's later version of the story clearly makes a baying Hecuba bestial in a far more horrific sense, but Euripides' ending seems harder to pin down. The doglike Erinyes in Aeschylus' *Eumenides* gouge out eyes (186), but they can transform under Athena's influence into kindly protectors of justice. One Euripidean fragment (TrGF 62h), probably from Euripides' lost *Alexander*, apparently has Cassandra predict that Hecuba will become a dog, the *agalma* (monument) of fire-bearing Hekate. The goddess Hekate is a deity ambiguously linked with dogs, childbirth, and with the underworld.[38] Clearly Hecuba in Polymestor's prophecy will literally enact a tragic fall; she will no longer survive as part of a civilized world and she has become indifferent to the pain of

Polymestor; yet, no longer a slave, she will also survive to protect others from disaster with fiery eyes/fire signs.[39] 'Hecabe's completed act of vengeance shows the way,' Burnett argues, since Kynossema, 'marks the place where men must change course as they move from wild justice towards a tamer kind, and as such it is a *tekmar*, an indication of ultimate design.'[40]

6

The Role of the Chorus

The chorus of Hecuba consists of Trojan women who identify themselves as supporters of Hecuba from the first moment of their entrance, where they arrive in haste, having taken the risk of leaving their own tents, to warn Hecuba about Polyxena's fate. In this first chanted narrative (the chorus uses the anapestic meter often used for entrances), the equivalent of a messenger speech, it expresses the kind of direct sympathy for Hecuba that it maintains throughout the play when it speaks in *iambic trimeters*. Female choruses are typically closely identified with female protagonists in Greek tragedy. At the same time, this chorus is deeply concerned both with their own future as Greek slaves and with confronting their own past as Trojan women.

Although some choral odes, like this *parodos* or chanted entrance, closely respond to the events surrounding them, the other three choral *stasima*, which are both sung and danced between episodes, have in this play a freer relation to the scenes around them. It is important to remember that a Greek audience would expect a chorus to locate the events of the play in a broader historical and mythical as well as divine context, although they here retain their identity as women in a specific context. In this respect, they are not, as some earlier interpreters of the Greek chorus tried to argue, in any simple sense ideal spectators; as in the majority of Greek tragedies, choruses are often women, foreigners, slaves, or old men, who bring a perspective to the action which differs from that of the audience, which was predominantly citizen men of various ages.¹ Choral dance, song, and language, like other sung parts of the play, also operate on a higher, lyrical register than the spoken scenes. Yet in this play at least, their songs are less intense and emotional that those of Hecuba, Polyxena, and Polymestor except when they join Hecuba in shared song.

All three choral *stasima* are preoccupied with the sea voyage this group of wives and mothers are about to undertake, express anxiety over their own fate, and share a sense of collective grief over the fall of their city.² The first *stasimon* (445–83) takes place after Polyxena departs for her sacrifice leaving her mother collapsed in grief on the stage and ends as Talthybius arrives to tell Hecuba about her daughter's death and to summon her to help with her burial. Polyxena is unwilling to accept the humiliating lot of slavery; this chorus, however, is instead concerned with their survival and their journey to other Greek cities.³ Will the ocean breeze ferry them to a Dorian land, such as that occupied by Agamemnon and Menelaus in Sparta, to fertile Phthia in Thessaly, Achilles' and Neoptolemus' homeland, or to an island like Delos, where the palm and the laurel held out their branches to support the goddess Leto, as she labored to bear Apollo and Artemis, or to Athens? Although the women know they are doomed to a pitiable indoor life as slaves, they wonder whether they will join maidens celebrating Artemis on Delos or weave the *peplos* (robe) for Athena's statue in the attic Parthenon, which displays Zeus laying to rest with his thunderbolt the Giants revolting against his regime. The mention of this divine fire seems to bring them back once again to their own fate as women who have lost children, fathers, and a country now smoking with dying flames. They imagine, as they did at the opening of their song, their journey from Asia and the 'halls of Hades' (presumably death or the world of the dead to which their city had been reduced) to the foreign lands of Europe. Each choral ode in Greek tragedy matches a strophe or turn in the dance to an antistrophe with the same meter, music, and perhaps choreography. Whereas the first strophic pair smoothly links possible points on a journey (444–65), the abrupt turn in this second strophic pair (466–83) from weaving the story of divine justice at Athens in the strophe to their own catastrophic losses at Troy in the antistrophe perhaps create a painful performed dissonance between their own reality and that of the Athenian audience.

At the center of this song, the chorus briefly identify not with their own role of wives and mothers, but with virgins who sing or weave for the virgin goddess Artemis in Delos and for Athena in Athens. Their wish is impossible, perhaps expressing a longing for the life of a citizen maiden on the verge of adulthood, free to engage in public worship and to display their skills as lovely singers, dancers, and weavers in orderly and stable rites that honor the gods.[4] It also represents their repeated identification in their choral stasima with Greek women, even though they themselves are barbarians. In this respect, they are like Hecuba in her earlier scenes, when she tries to cross barbarian–Greek boundaries, and also implicitly respond to Odysseus' complaint that Hecuba has failed to recognize the suffering of the Greeks left at home to lament the dead at Troy. Sung in an *aeolo-choriambic*, typically lyrical meter, the chorus' language creates through its decorative imagery a vivid imaginary journey to concrete places and rituals. Here the women become in imagination part of an ideal community.

The second stasimon (629–57) is sung after Hecuba's speech in which she meditates on Polyxena's death and on human fate and enters the tent to find ornaments for Polyxena's burial. At its conclusion, the maidservant sent to fetch water for the burial enters with the body of Polydorus, covered in elaborate, if perhaps frayed, Trojan robes. In response to Hecuba's theme, the chorus now meditates in a flashback on the fate of both themselves and all Trojans, whose doom began with Paris' crossing of the sea to abduct Helen (629–37). The antistrophe (638–48), which moves from Paris and Helen to the collective Trojan disaster, links the beauty of the brilliant Helen with that of the three goddesses whose beauty contest the shepherd Paris judged, since both occur in the same structural position in their matched song.[5] (Paris' choice of Aphrodite over Hera and Athena led to the abduction of Helen.) Their thoughts now spill over in an unusual fashion to the epode of this stasimon (649–56), which has no matching metrical section, as Paris' choices spill over into war and ruin for his city and finally to a lamenting Spartan girl and an aged mother who has lost children as well.[6] The meter adds some iambic rhythms to the aeolic rhythms of the first stasimon and the ode's interlacing word order reinforces the chorus' concern with an encircling fate that binds Greeks and Trojans and concludes by bridging the gap between friend and foe that remains a concern in the action as well.[7] The ode is framed by Hecuba's own maternal losses, as she moves from grief over her daughter to anguish over the discovery of her son. This ode enhances the enormity of the women's collective losses.

The third stasimon (905–52) intervenes between the maidservant's exit to bring Polymestor and his sons to Hecuba's tent and the appearance of the three Thracians. The chorus' focus is now on its own experience of the fall of Troy. Here the meter is *dactylo-epitrite*, a high-style choral meter which merges the dactylic meter of epic and aeolic and iambo-trochaic rhythms, as well as, thematically, past and present, and is associated with an elaborate choral style that emphasizes vivid narrative.[8] The first strophe (905–13) evokes the sacked city of Troy, surrounded by armed Greeks, shorn of towers and disfigured by smoke. The antistrophe (914–22) matches a city ravaged like a woman in the strophe with a Trojan woman falling asleep after festivities celebrating the supposed departure of the Greeks from Troy; the woman lies by her husband, who has hung up his weapon and feels free from care. The matching strophes ominously link the time immediately before and during the fall of Troy in performance.

In the second strophe (923–32), a Trojan woman binds her hair while gazing into a golden mirror as she prepares for bed. She suddenly hears the shout of the attacking Greeks, whom the audience knows have been hidden in the Trojan horse. In the antistrophe (933–42), the woman, dressed in a single garment like a Spartan girl (not the more modest dress of a matron) leaves her marriage bed to supplicate the goddess Artemis to no avail. She is carried to the ships after seeing her husband killed, and as she looks back to the city with grief her emotion spills over into an epode (as in the second stasimon), as she curses Helen and Paris who were the source of her troubles and hopes Helen (too) will never reach home. (Hecuba had earlier wished for the destruction of Helen, 441–3.)[9] Helen haunts the chorus like an avenging spirit or *alastôr*; an *alastôr* earlier seized Hecuba when she discovered her dead son, just as the chorus woman saw her own husband dead and presumably left unburied.[10] This reawakened spirit of revenge is about to be embodied in the revenge of Hecuba and the other Trojan women hidden in her tent. The chorus follow Polymestor's exit into the tent with a brief astrophic song presaging his just doom that is dominated by excited dochmiacs (1023–34). In short, the chorus, whose songs are more wide-ranging and detached from the moment in the choral stasima, ends by actively sharing and wanting to support Hecuba's sense of divinely supported justice (1030, 1042–3, 1085–7), defending women against Polymestor's slurs (1183–6), and praising Hecuba's arguments as if the women were now an authoritative political body (1238–9): 'Fine actions always afford a starting point for fine argument!'

7

Sizing up Revenge Tragedy

As we have seen, modern critics disagree in their interpretation of *Hecuba*. Yet previous eras interpreted the play quite differently. Before reaching any conclusions, it is important to examine how the play's earlier reception can help to interpret it. The Greeks gave us the first great revenge tragedies of the Western tradition, although this theme clearly goes back in Greek tradition at least to the Homeric epics. Odysseus' successful revenge plot against the villainous Ithacan suitors prefigures many aspects of the later Greek plays, although the outcome of the epic gives justice and survival to the hero and death to his enemies. Orestes' revenge for his father Agamemnon's death is explicitly held up as an example to Odysseus' son Telemachus in the *Odyssey* and then serves as a central plot in tragedies by Aeschylus, Sophocles, and Euripides. Among Euripides' extant plays, *Medea*, *Electra*, *Orestes* (the plot against Helen), or even *Bacchae* could be characterized as revenge tragedies, and *Phoenician Women*, *Andromache*, *Hippolytus*, *The Children of Heracles*, *Heracles*, *Ion*, and *Trojan Women* all include characters desiring or enacting revenge. Revenge tragedies continued to be in vogue in the ancient world, from the Roman tragedies of Seneca at the infamous court of Nero to the Byzantine period, where *Hecuba* and *Orestes* became two of the most carefully preserved and copied Euripidean tragedies. If the revenge theme was not a reason for preserving these plays, it certainly did not impede their preservation.

Greeks—philosophers like Plato excepted—certainly had no qualms about admitting that revenge is both sweet and justifiable. The popular creed 'do good to your friends and bad to your enemies' never went out of fashion. On this principle, honor, status, and even justice depended. As Aristotle remarks in his *Rhetoric* (1367a24), 'To take vengeance on one's enemies is nobler than to come to terms with them; for to retaliate is just, and that which is just is noble; and further, a courageous man ought not to allow himself to be beaten.'[1] Homer's Achilles says in the *Iliad* that vengeful anger swarms like smoke in a man's heart, sweeter by far than the dripping of honey (18.108–10). Homer's aged Hecuba, as mentioned earlier, wishes she could set her teeth in the middle of Achilles' liver and eat it because he killed her son Hector and dragged his body around the city walls (*Iliad* 24.212–13). Apollo commands Orestes to avenge his father's death in Aeschylus' *Oresteia*; if he fails his father's Furies will pursue him. Thucydides' Gylippus argues to the Syracusans before their battle with the Athenian invaders: 'let us engage in anger, convinced that, as between adversaries, nothing is more legitimate than to claim to sate the whole wrath of one's soul in punishing the aggressor, and nothing more sweet, as the proverb has it, than vengeance upon an enemy, which will now be ours to take' (7.68).[2] Although in the classical period trial by jury replaced the familial vendettas of myth, 'not only are enmity and revenge accepted as natural motives for a lawsuit, but the language of revenge came to be used for legal punishment, while litigation is often treated as a legalized revenge.'[3] Even Plato's Protagoras, who objects to what he sees as a widespread practice of 'taking irrational vengeance (*timôria*) like a wild beast' and punishing to avenge past offenses, recognizes the value of punishment to deter future wrongs (*Protagoras* 324a–c). In certain respects at least, the grim symmetry of Hecuba's revenge in Euripides' play might well have appealed to a well-developed connoisseurship about revenge in its original audience. At the very least, as Judith Mossman argues, 'It should be clear that a mere statement to take revenge cannot be construed on its own as a symptom of a deteriorating character."[4]

Malcolm Heath's valuable discussion of the critical reception of the play from Antiquity to the present makes clear that evaluating *Hecuba*'s critical reception is unusually important to its interpretation.[5] The scattered responses to *Hecuba* in Antiquity are hard to pin down and less helpful in addressing this issue. The play's opening, the dignity of Polyxena's response and the messenger's report of her heroic death, Hecuba's laments, her prostitution of her daughter, her philosophizing, the pathos of her double loss, and minor issues of dramatic plausibility all received response or mention in ancient authors or in scholia (ancient notes to the plays), but the play's edifying rhetorical content and its frequent gnomes concerning justice, persuasion, good breeding, and fortune attracted the most attention.[6]

For the Renaissance, *Hecuba* was the first Greek tragedy to be read by students in the original, the most widely translated at an early date into Latin and vernacular languages, and the first to receive an actual performance. Leonizio Pilato, who taught Greek to Petrarch and Boccaccio, made a partial interlinear Latin translation in 1362. Desiderius Erasmus published a widely read Latin translation based on the 1503 Aldine edition of Marcus Musurus in 1506 with *Iphigenia in Aulis* and Melanchthon produced the play in the Low Countries (Belgium) sometime between 1506 and 1514 and in 1525 at Wittenberg.[7] Other Latin and seven vernacular translations in Spanish, Italian, and French proliferated in the sixteenth century after Erasmus.[8] Gasparus Stiblinus, translator and editor of the first Greek-Latin volume of Euripides' compete works (1562), attributed to it the first place among Greek tragedies.[9]

For those unfamiliar with *Hecuba* itself, Ovid's popular *Metamorphoses* (13. 399–575) closely echoes Euripides' play by including Polymestor's impious murder of Polydorus, Achilles' ghostly appearance in Thrace, Polyxena's noble speech and heroic death, and

Hecuba's revenge on Polymestor; in Ovid's version Hecuba's laments over her dead daughter expand on Euripides and her transformation into a dog immediately follows her gouging out of Polymestor's eyes with her bare hands and a Thracian counterattack on the queen. Despite this horrific conclusion, Ovid closes the episode with a neutral (or tongue in cheek?) assessment: 'Her sad fortune touched the Trojans and her Grecian foes and all the gods as well; yes, all, even Juno, sister and wife of Jove, declared that Hecuba had not deserved such an end.' (573–5).[10] Other Renaissance readers might have been familiar with the Trojan hero Aeneas' encounter with the spirit of the murdered Polydorus at his burial mound in Thrace (*Aeneid* 3, 41–68).

Renaissance critics were also strongly influenced by Aristotle's *Poetics* and Senecan tragedy, including the Roman playwright's own *Troades*, which despite its emphasis on Polyxena's sacrifice and Hecuba's paradigmatic maternal grief bears little relation to Euripides' *Hecuba* or *Trojan Women*; for example, Seneca features the death of Astyanax rather than that of Polydorus.[11] They admired *Hecuba* not only for its paradigmatic representation of the pitiful fragility of human fortunes, but for its horrific, triumphant, and bloody revenge by a frustrated victim seeking retribution for a crime that has gone unpunished, as well as for its compelling rhetoric. For these Renaissance critics, horror, violence, moral depravity, and emotional extremity constituted a desirable dramatic *atrocitas* (tragic horror). English revenge tragedy through the 1640s featured ghosts, revenge that exceeded the original crime by creating new victims, descent into madness, foreign settings and foreign avengers, savaged bodies, abused virgins, deceitful plotting, and a play within a play.[12] Revenge alone was thought to restore the grieving to some kind of health or equilibrium. *Hecuba*'s ghost is not vindictive (Polydorus simply wants burial), the heroine, who is far more virtuous and decisive than most avengers, is not specifically defined as mad, her various questionable opponents are not represented primarily as tyrants, and her carefully-staged and ingenious revenge plot is not metatheatrical.[13] Yet the Renaissance revival of Greek plays like *Hecuba* by humanist scholars clearly played a role in developing this popular genre and resonated with it.

The play's plot, which from the Renaissance perspective displayed a clear sequential Aristotelian unity, offered a pleasing *varietas* (variety); additional episodes such as the death of Polyxena did not detract at this period from but enhanced this feature. Sir Philip Sydney's *Apologie for Poetrie* (c. 1581, published posthumously in 1595) specifically offered it as an example of a well-constructed tragedy.[14] Finally, Hecuba's exemplary misfortunes and Polymestor's just, deserved fate proved both instructive and pleasurable (the play demonstrated *utilitas*, utility).[15] If anything, J. C. Scaliger even thought the ending too upbeat, since Hecuba suffered less at the end than at the beginning.[16]

Hecuba's revenge itself was never criticized at this period as excessive and her poised execution of her retaliation could even receive praise; its rhetoric would no doubt have appealed as much to the Renaissance as it did to late Antiquity.[17] In addition, editions, vernacular translations, and documented stagings of Euripidean or Sophoclean plays before 1600 overwhelmingly featured female protagonists (Euripides' *Iphigenia in Aulis, Medea, Alcestis, Phoenician Women, Trojan Women, Electra*, as well as Sophocles' *Antigone* and *Electra*.) Both *Hecuba* and *Iphigenia in Aulis* (the second most popular Greek tragedy of the period, translated into English by Lady Jane Lumley c. 1550–3) featured passionately bereaved mothers and sacrificial daughters.[18]

Seventeenth- and eighteenth-century writers, however, began to object to any episode they viewed as not causally integrated into the tragic plot like the Polyxena episode; a focus on the fortunes of a single tragic figure (arguably the case for Hecuba) also came to be viewed as increasingly desirable. Extreme bloodshed and horror, and even bad characters, ceased to define their conception of the tragic. Since Polymestor's unmitigated wickedness was no longer viewed as fundamentally generative of tragic pity and fear, the second half of *Hecuba* began to attract disapproval. The nineteenth century went on to fault the play for lacking the free exercise of a unified character and spiritual elevation in the face of necessity (rather than chance, as in much of Euripides) to be expected of tragedy. Only Polyxena rather than Hecuba could be said to live up to these new standards.[19]

As we have seen, modern critics have tended to follow post-sixteenth-century critics in finding the play's plot structure problematic, and often looked to the unifying figure of Hecuba and her moral degradation under pressure for thematic unity. Justice for the powerless (women, slaves, foreigners) or horrific revenge is now no longer thought necessarily alien to tragedy as a form (to say nothing of opera, the novel, or twentieth-century vigilante films—one might cite Clint Eastwood's *Unforgiven* or the Macedonian film *Before the Rain*). Yet Hecuba's revenge, despite specific claims to justice in the text, has rarely been thought by modern critics to represent genuine justice in divine or human form.[20]

This reception history suggests, however, that in contradiction to the considerable modern criticism of the play's unity and characterization, or the supposed marring of its pathos by excessive brutality, ancient readers/audiences, like Renaissance critics, could have looked to the play as both acceptably tragic and rich with rhetorical and gnomic authority. (Aristotelian views on dramatic unity had in any case not yet been published for the original viewers of *Hecuba*.) In many respects, what has stood out in the close analysis I have tried to offer are the play's rhetorical/philosophical confrontations so admired in Antiquity and the Renaissance. Every major character in the play attempts and generally fails to persuade others of the correctness of their rational views and tries to act on those seemingly irreconcilable views. Hecuba begins with a traditionally aristocratic view closely linked with her own situation. Her fierce sense of justice does not change, but her repertoire of argument continually enlarges until in her last speech she is able to argue (for better or worse) more as a politician than as a wronged, formerly elite individual or philosopher of traditional morality. She even relieves Agamemnon of the burden of Polymestor's role as ally to the Greeks by defining him as an enemy and gives him the ethical language to authorize his condemnation. If, as some argue, her character does in any way descend through enacting violence, her language and her claim to justice ascend and are increasingly corroborated by her opponents.

Concluding Analysis of the Play

As John Kerrigan has argued in his book *Revenge Tragedy*, the plots of revenge tragedies require avengers to imitate in some way those who wronged them and to involve the innocent in their retribution. They are inevitably characterized by 'a mimetic againness (re-venge, re-tribution, re-cognition).'[21] Though each revenge is meant to set a limit to violence and can invite an audience to enjoy the disadvantaged avenger's success, the act generally leads to further violence and some form of moral vacancy. These vengeful acts demand the public judgment that they receive in *Hecuba* even more than tragic pity and fear. Yet 'Revenge tragedies ... can explore the intractable question of whether rhetoric disentangles problems, or is, in the worse sort of way, a moral solvent.'[22] The unending repetition of violence in *Hecuba* and the struggle to respond to it in persuasive language invites similar exploration. The desire for revenge lies behind any system of justice, and it often becomes explosive when subjugated groups feel that they have no real access to formal justice and power. Whatever we think about the repercussions of Hecuba's revenge, the play also invites its audience to listen repeatedly to her arguments for *dikê* and *nomos*, and to take at least temporary pleasure in her ingenious defeat of Polymestor and at her final success in publically defending what she views as justice.

In this revenge plot, Euripides puts Hecuba and the Trojan women at the moral center of their dramatic world. Indeed, as Froma Zeitlin has argued, Hecuba is 'the only standard bearer for an objective moral order' in the play.[23] She tries to unite divine and human justice with an aristocratic sense of reciprocity in a world not concerned or able to reconcile them. As I have argued elsewhere, Euripides tends to put the defense of traditional laws in the hands of older, philosophizing, maternal women.[24] It may also be worth noting here that although Aristotle and others could find philosophizing women inappropriate, a scholion at *Hecuba* 601 finds Hecuba's philosophizing appropriate to a character of royal status.[25] (Sophocles, by contrast, gives the defense of the rites of burial to the virginal Antigone or to Odysseus in *Ajax*.) In her failed arbitration of the quarrel of her sons Eteocles and Polyneices in *Phoenician Women*, Jocasta argues for honoring the cosmic principle of equality, which binds friends, cities, and allies (535–8) and is by nature lawful for humans, whereas inequality breeds hatred. Theseus' mother Aethra in *Suppliant Women* persuades her son to defend the burial of the dead seven against Thebes on the grounds of Panhellenic tradition. Hecuba bases her pleas for justice on principles that she views as universal to social order and finally, to political self-interest as well. I have argued elsewhere that the choice of women to defend such traditional laws reflects an increasingly marginalized status for these laws during the Peloponnesian War.[26] But it also reflects women's separation from public life and their particular vulnerability to violence and chance. Women, even more than men, depend on oaths, supplication, rules governing hospitality, the powers of persuasion. Their roles in caring for children and the dead allow them to bridge past and future and they bring with them ideological links to nature, children, suffering, pity, and domestic worlds. Hence they logically can, like Hecuba, merge in their pleas a contextually-oriented morality with an appeal to ancestral traditions. By contrast, the men of this play rely on formal bonds between the formally equal. For them, advantage (including gold) and political expediency/the interests of the collective take precedence over altruism and pity.[27] Though capable of pity like Agamemnon and committed to public values like Odysseus, they do not choose to act on or claim the principles defended by Hecuba unless they are finally adopting her own positions, like Agamemnon at the end of her trial speech.

In Greek tragedy generally, some of the best and most authoritative roles on the Attic stage were designed for women of all ages (although acted by men). By giving an authoritative voice to Hecuba and Polyxena, two barbarian, female, former enemies, the play raises difficult questions about Athens and its own ills. For us, the equivalent might be an American play about the aftermath of the Vietnam War in which the characters with the most serious claim to moral authority in speech were Vietnamese women whose lives and human rights were destroyed by the war. Hecuba's bewilderment about Polymestor's crime is all too similar to that expressed by Bosnian Muslims when former neighbors came to treat them as candidates for ethnic cleansing. In the ancient world, revenge tragedy clearly spoke to the war-torn population of Athens. Yet the complexity and brilliance of *Hecuba*'s arguments capture something important, and perhaps more important, about our own realities as well.

8

Performances of *Hecuba*

Pre-twentieth-century Performances

As noted earlier, a few Renaissance productions of *Hecuba* almost immediately followed the publication of Erasmus' Latin translation in Belgium at the Collège du Porc (1506–1514) and at Wittenberg, Germany (1525).[1] French adaptations of parts of the play began in 1579, with *La Troade*, a version based on Euripides and Seneca, and the loosely related *Polyxène* in 1584. An Italian opera version in Venice, *Le Rovine di Troia* (1707), and a *Polidoro* by Antonio Lotti in Venice in 1715 preceded two London productions, Richard West's *Hecuba* of 1726 and John Delap's 1761 adaptation of the play.[2] Another mixture of Euripides' and Seneca's versions in Germany, the 1736 *Hekuba*, revised as *Troianerinnen* and directed by Johann Elias Schlegel, was followed in France by a 1792 version at the Comédie Française and a 1793 translation at the Théâtre de la Nation in Paris. In the 1800s, a French opera version (1800), Greek productions (1817, 1856, 1866, 1867, 1887, 1896), and Richard Valpy's 1827 *Hecuba* at the Reading School in England were performed along with a burlesque by Cranstoun Metcalfe, *Hecuba à la mode: or The Wily Greek and the Modest Maid* (London 1893).[3] The early 1900s saw numerous productions in Greece and scattered productions in Poland (1916), American colleges, and Italy, including a first production by the Istituto Nazionale del Dramma Antico at the famous Italian festival in Siracusa (1939 with later performances in 1962, 1998, and 2006). Interest in the play in many more venues has radically increased since the 1970s.

Twentieth- and Twenty-first-century Performances

Euripides' better known *Trojan Women* has frequently appealed to twentieth- and twenty-first-century audiences, especially in response to numerous wars; the play invites pity for its helpless, enslaved women and their lost city, and predicts as well future suffering for the victors. *Hecuba*, on the other hand, focuses sharply on the ways that war corrupts both victor and victim, and stresses the role that corrupt language and political change play in this process. The recent, if more limited, turn to *Hecuba* seems to suggest a new willingness to take on more complex views of war and its after effects through Greek tragedy and, in the case of the United States at least, to confront a deep-seated American fascination and discomfort with rhetoric. What follows examines a selection of some important productions of the original, adaptations, and new versions in the twentieth- and twenty-first centuries in English that are especially well documented and represent different interpretations of the play in performance.

Turning to *Hecuba* to capture the corrupting effects of war predates late twentieth-century developments. In the United States Henry Bertram Lister's pre-Second World War (1938) *The Bride of a Ghost* or *Polyxena*, a new version for the La Bohème Club of San Francisco that framed some of the major scenes of Euripides' *Trojan Women* with the story of Hecuba, Polyxena, and Polydorus from *Hecuba*, offered an even more negative view of the Trojans' fate than Euripides' play.[4] In this pessimistic version, Hecuba offered Odysseus her Trojan gold in order to save Polyxena and he was greedily prepared to take it; but Polymestor had gambled it away and then killed Polydorus, who revealed Polymestor's crime with his dying breath. The Greeks went on to stage a 'wedding' for the heroic Polyxena to Achilles' ghost that was denounced as a sacrilege by Cassandra (this scene was probably borrowed from the Roman poet Seneca's version, *Troades*). Hecuba was permitted by the Greeks to pronounce a punishment for Polymestor: death by stoning from her Trojan women. Hecuba, Cassandra, and Polyxena united at the conclusion of the play with the knowledge that they would soon meet after death. The play predicts that the greedy Greeks, whose primary motive for the war was gold, will go on to meet equally bad fates. This play very likely represents a response to one of the worst periods of unemployment during the Great Depression as well as to America's increasing fears of becoming involved in the Second World War.

A pointedly post-war and equally pessimistic version of *Hecuba*, performed by the Tokyo Amateur Dramatic Club as part of a trilogy called *The House of Atreus* by Burton Crane at the Exchange Hotel Theatre in Tokyo in 1949, was paired with abridged adaptations of Aeschylus' *Agamemnon* and Sophocles' *Electra* to produce a triple revenge tragedy that ended with the following choral lament that closed the play's version of *Electra*: 'The sons and daughters of a wicked king/Have written out in blood their tale of hate (Elektra sinks down on the steps, her hair screening her face. She sobs.) Are they delivered from their suffering?/Have they gained freedom from the hand of fate?/The answer from heaven is a No./O woe! O unimaginable woe!' (p. 87). Accordingly, this version entirely eliminated the more uplifting Polyxena episode to focus on Polydorus and Hecuba's revenge on a patently tyrannical Polymestor. The evil Polymestor's opening mirth at Hecuba, followed by an exchange of Nazi-style salutes with his followers, was later echoed by Hecuba after her revenge, and again by Polymestor as he predicts the death of Agamemnon. Crane's Hecuba ends with a desperate attempt to shrug off Polymestor's prophecy about her transformation into a dog. The published version of the trilogy includes music composed in the Dorian mode by Burton Crane and a description of set, colorful lighting, costumes, and acting styles; Jadwiga Babcock starred as Hecuba.[5]

Martha Graham's dance version, *Cortege of Eagles*, with settings by Isamu Noguchi, lighting by Jean Rosenthal, and music by Eugene Lester, merged parts of Euripides' *Trojan Women* with his *Hecuba*. Premiered in 1967, the dance has been re-performed in New York a number of times since, specially in the mid-1980s. The dance is presented as a flashback in the mind of the regal Hecuba (originally played in her seventies by Graham herself) and presided over by a deathlike figure (Charon) that holds and often deploys a curved mask with a red tongue over his white face as he introduces and encircles each of Hecuba's remembered Trojan dead. Helen, the only real survivor, arrogantly haunts the scene as the audience observes Priam put an enormous gold bracelet on Hecuba's arm as they pose before pillars representing an unfallen Troy. Duets between Paris and Helen and Hector and Andromache follow. Achilles attempts to abduct a resisting Polyxena and then kills Hector in a duel. Priam keeps his youngest son Polydorus from engaging in battle. The city's pillars fall. Andromache laments Hector's dead body before her son Astyanax.

The dance moves into present time. The now dead Achilles, lying on a black pallet, summons Polyxena, whose youthful solo ends as she opens the top of her red and white dress, takes a curved weapon from Achilles' hand, and bravely kills herself. Andromache tenderly covers Hecuba's eyes during this scene. Hecuba, placing her golden robe on the black triangle that covered the dead Polyxena, laments her daughter together with her last son Polydorus and then faces off with Helen. A military dance begins, led by Polydorus and Hector's son Astyanax; Polymestor, played by the dancer who played Achilles, intervenes, kills Polydorus, and abandons the body after taking gold from around his neck. Helen arrogantly steps over the dead Polydorus. The dancer who played Hector appears as a new Charon-like figure in a white mask shaped like a geometric keyhole. Soldiers then carry off the dead Astyanax, followed by his lamenting mother Andromache, as Hecuba gestures in prayer and approaches the body of Polydorus. Observed by the Charon figure, who stands on a small platform above the action like a deity of revenge, the chorus of five Trojan Women in black, who have been linked with their queen from the opening of the dance, then cover the boy's body.[6] Polymestor enters, pretending sorrow at Hecuba's lot. Offering him her gold bracelet, Hecuba lures him into a space created by a dark blue and black cloth held by the chorus women. They entrap him in its folds as Hecuba removes a large curved gold brooch and wildly stabs Polymestor's eyes. She leads the staggering blinded king to Polydorus' body; at the touch of the young man's face Polymestor recedes in horror. Finally, to a powerful musical accompaniment, Hecuba seats herself, cradles the gold brooch in her arms and in the folds of her dress like a child. A ghostly parade of her dead walks by. She raises a clawlike hand before her bleak, masklike face.[7]

Although Graham had used a heroine's film-like flashback as a unifying device in her 1958 *Clytemnestra*, she seems more directly inspired in this case by Euripides himself, whose *Hecuba* begins with the queen reporting her nightmare after Polydorus' ghostly appearance and ends with her completed revenge. Graham's Polyxena presents a suicidal variation on the princess's noble death in Euripides' messenger speech, including a symbolic display of her breasts; the flashback had previously included an incident representing Achilles' previous desire for her known in variant myths. Graham's version pointedly deletes the horrific killing of Polymestor's children (as she also did in her dance version of Euripides' *Medea, Cave of the Heart*), but visualizes Helen's verbal haunting of both the enraged Hecuba and the chorus in Euripides' *Hecuba*.[8]

A 1987 professional performance for Manara Productions of *Hecuba*, directed by Lamis Khalaf at the Powerhouse Theater in Santa

Monica, California identified the Trojans with the Palestinians, the
Thracians with the Lebanese, and the Greeks with Israelis; the gods
were the current superpowers. Some reviewers responded positively
to its assertive representation of the dispossessed.[9] The most important
American production, and very likely the single most successful
performance of the original play, soon followed. I have chosen for this
reason to discuss this one production in much more detail. Carey
Perloff directed two productions of *Hekabe* (the original Greek title)
at the American Conservatory Theater in San Francisco at the Yerba
Buena Center in 1995 and at the Geary Theater in 1998. The 1998
version was also performed at the Williamstown Theater Festival in
Williamstown, Massachusetts. Both versions starred Olympia Dukakis
as Hekabe to great acclaim (**Figure 3**). This performance established a
Balkan background for the production by using a professional Eastern
European a cappella group, KITKA, as a chorus for which David Lang
composed music. This chorus, already experienced as a chorus and
well acquainted with the contemporary plight of refugees, served to
underline the bonding among the women of this play, and offered the
single most powerful choral performance of any production of
Hecuba known to me. The tough, modern translation by Timberlake
Wertenbaker underlined feminist issues, both female subjugation by
male leaders and women's surprising capacity to act collectively and
re-write history. As Perloff put it in her director's notes, Euripides
'relentlessly examined the chaos generated when rhetoric that
supports a democratic legal system no longer matches the reality most
of us perceive around us. Suddenly Hecuba's complex issues of gender
conflict and moral responsibility stood vividly in this foreground ...
Written in wartime about wartime ... [the play] looks at what happens
when men take advantage of their physical prowess and power to
betray women who depend on them for survival and for justice. It
reveals the psychological devastation that follows a morally
indefensible war, and it lifts the veil of "privacy" to reveal what happens

Figure 3. Olympia Dukakis as Hekabe with the Chorus Leader, Remi Barclay Bosseau, in *Hekabe*, directed by Carey Perloff in 1995, American Conservatory Theater, Yerba Buena Center, San Francisco. Courtesy of the American Conservatory Theater. Photograph by Ken Friedman.

when sex and politics intertwine. Most importantly, it asks, Who is allowed to write history?'

The 1998 version of *Hekabe* framed a narrow strip at the front of the stage with a sloping ramp and wooden drawbridge on stage right and ragged tents for the women on stage left. Above the ramp was a furled sail that unfurled at the opening, when the ghost of Polymestor was projected on it, and began to lower again as the wind picked up at the conclusion. At the end of the ramp was a pit from which Hecuba emerged in the eerie darkness of the opening scene. Polydorus' opening speech was, in contrast to Euripides, interrupted by Hecuba's report of her dream. After Polydorus disappeared, the sky lightened and gradually became a sullen orange as the play went on. Hecuba's outraged response to the news of Polyxena's fate, 'Where are the words?' followed by a low growl, set the tone for the queen's struggle to articulate her sense of violated justice throughout the play. Dukakis exploited Hekabe's double identity as former queen and slave. With Odysseus she began with a slave's deferential request, supplicated an Odysseus who kept establishing his distance from her, yet towered to her full voice height as she asked to be both heard and seen making her case for the law. A moment of doubt struck her when Odysseus, demanding her gaze in return, made his central argument for Polyxena's sacrifice. In her scene with Polyxena Hekabe angrily resisted and failed to accept her daughter's free consent to her sacrifice. She never stopped struggling actively to hold her back. 'I am living my death now,' she insisted. Her mesmerized response to Talthybius' speech about Polyxena's death gave way to immediate despair since her meditation about the role of noble birth and education in producing her daughter's heroism was cut.

On her recognition of the dead Polydorus, a spirit slowly seized Hekabe's body, which visibly shook with outrage. A relatively sympathetic Agamemnon listened to her plea for justice while she embraced the body of the dead Polydorus. Then, as she shifted to trying to take advantage of Agamemnon's relation to Cassandra in a more feminine seductive voice, she crossed the stage to speak to him standing among the chorus women, whose unity, shared glances, and supplication of Agamemnon anticipated their later share in her revenge. As has often been the case in many recent productions, the audience's laughter at Hekabe's deception of Polymestor, and the chorus women's flirtatious disarming, partial undressing, and anointing of Polymestor before he entered the tent, along with their later cat and mouse game with the blind king, implicated them powerfully in the successful revenge. Polymestor's dead children were in this production represented by puppets, which helped maintain a degree of sympathy for Hekabe. With a last burst of energy, Hekabe made her public case for justice while again holding the body of Polydorus 'with a face resembling a tragic mask'[10] and departed in a rising wind to bury her children while showing little interest in Polymestor's prophecy. This play opened with

Dukakis emerging from a pit on stage and closed with her stunned remark that 'History has no compassion.'

Although both productions were above all lauded for the extraordinary, nuanced performance of Olympia Dukakis as Hekabe, which grew over time to unify the play more effectively,[11] reviewers found themselves responding almost with relief to the play's turn from suffering to revenge in the final scenes.[12] As many of these critics understood, the struggle to win justice, whether with words or in the last resort through violence, was central to the performance. 'It examines what the politics of necessity does to both the arbiters of war and its victims. It is retribution at its rawest.'[13] '*Hecuba* is a revenge tragedy at its cruelest, based on the ethical code of ancient Greece. Those ethics still resonate today. When was the last time you saw or heard someone proclaim "No justice, no peace," on the evening news?'[14] Dukakis herself argued in an interview that 'Justice is a political issue ... An act for personal gain was considered revenge. If you did something to cleanse the world of an abomination, it was justice.'[15] Although this production cut small sections of the play's debates and long speeches by Hecuba, reviews could still complain, however, as they had concerning US productions of Greek tragedy from the early twentieth century, about the 'inevitable declamatory passages and lack of stage action.'[16]

The African Continuum Theater Company's (ACTCo) 1998 performance in Washington, DC, directed by African-American Jennifer Nelson using a published translation by her sister, the poet Marilyn Nelson, focused instead on the slavery theme (both Greek and American) and Hecuba's outraged motherhood rather than justice.[17] The close translation was influenced by African women's slave narratives and the language was colored in places by the well known spiritual, 'Nobody Knows the Trouble I've Seen'; the last choral speech alluded to Robert Hayden's poem 'Middle Passage.' Both the music (rainsticks, drum, and calabash) and the rhetorical style were influenced by African and African-American traditions. The male characters were depersonalized by wearing masks. In this context, the play's slavery themes took on a new and dominant resonance in lines such as: 'I'll die before I'll be a slave' (Polyxena, p. 94); 'a cold comfort comes/from knowing how free you were/as you died;' 'Master,/let a slave/set you free from fear;' 'Can language name my loss?' (all Hecuba, pp. 104, 120, 84). Cheryl Collins, in a performance of Hecuba broadly recognized as brilliant, rang the changes from pain and passionate persuasion to a powerful concluding legal brief for her revenge.

The period 2004–5 saw a striking number of British and American productions of Hecuba that responded to the Iraq War. Jonathan Kent's 2004 production of a version by Frank McGuinness (based on a literal translation by Fionnuala Murphy) at London's Donmar Warehouse opened with the play's single aged chorus member painting names of actual victims of war on a rough brick wall at the back of the stage. Polydorus' ghost arose miraculously from a pool of water set between a sloping beach and the audience that reflected light on the back wall. Sizzling lights accompanied the entrances of the contemptuous, patronizing, hypocritical or equivocal Greek generals garbed in dark suits symbolic of their power. Polymestor entered wearing colonial British garb accompanied by his two British-style school children. Once blinded and wearing a masklike, bleeding face, he crawled sniffing out Hecuba like a dog. The play closed with the once elegant women passing around plastic bags containing the body parts of Polymestor's dead children to a soundscape of a howling dog. Hecuba herself was left scrabbling doglike in the sand.

Both the intimacy of this production and McGuiness' idiomatic, visceral translation[18] stressed how quickly civilization can be short-circuited by wars even after their supposed conclusion. The chorus' assertion 'Times change, so do we/Friends turn to foes/That's the world' underlined an important motif in this performance. At the end Agamemnon ironically asserted that 'now we can go home, the war is over.' Yet the violent treatment of the children's bodies and Hecuba's

Figure 4. Clare Higgins as Hecuba in a version of *Hecuba* by Frank McGuinness based on a literal translation by Fionnuala Murphy, directed in 2004 by Jonathan Kent at the Donmar Warehouse, London, England.

bestial final posture suggested otherwise.[19] The imperious rage of this Hecuba, played to considerable acclaim by the Olivier award-winning Clare Higgins (**Figure 4**), was described in the program notes as 'a destructive meltdown;'[20] in the end her rage surpassed her earlier terror, tenderness, and pain. As one critic remarked: 'It used to be considered a weakness that for half the play, Hecuba is a victim, and for the other half a tyrant: that at one moment she is wracked by grief, and at the next fired up by fury. This now seems a strength, a demonstration of the non-Christian truth that pain and sorrow are as likely to degrade as to ennoble.'[21]

In 2005, Laurence Boswell directed a translation by the poet Tony Harrison[22] starring Vanessa Redgrave for the Royal Shakespeare

Company at the Albery Theatre in London; the play, now directed by Harrison, later moved to the US (New York at the Brooklyn Academy of Music and Washington, DC at the Kennedy Center) and to Delphi, Greece. This controversial production highlighted a chorus of twelve barefoot women dressed in headscarves and long blue and green robes who sang music drawing on Middle Eastern tonalities by Mick Sands and accompanied by cello, percussion, and keyboards. Although some critics responded positively to the music, for others it suggested contemporary musicals—'Hecuba the Musical' one called it.[23] The set's neutral beige cylinders, textured to resemble grooved concrete, revolved for exits and entrances; this set was replaced in the US by crowded rows of military tents labeled US and UK. Harrison's percussive, alliterative blank verse translation overdid references to the Iraq War in the view of many critics.[24] 'The coalition vote elects your daughter as the dedication for Achilles' tomb' or Polyxena's 'I'll spin it again so that we're all clear' offer two examples. Polymestor called the women 'terrorists from Troy.' Darrell D'Silva's accent as Odysseus suggested George Bush. Arguably, however, this language was aimed at drawing attention to the abuses of human rights and democratic procedures by the Greek generals instead of emphasizing 'the revenge of an indigenous population against foreign forces.'[25] Redgrave's frail, tottering, defeated, wild-haired Hecuba was consistently restrained. Even during her revenge she produced no more than a grim, sardonic smile. Her passionless, remote, perhaps deliberately soulless Hecuba, whose relation to this version's highly performative chorus remained cryptic, nevertheless maintained a ruthless ability to calculate strategically. 'If you allow the law to be corrupted and nothing's done to punish those who kill their guests, and violate holy places, there's no safe center in the lives of men,' she argued fiercely to Agamemnon.

This production was in fact a partial reprise of a much more successful production directed by Boswell in 1992 at London's Gate Theatre using a translation by Kenneth McLeish.[26] The twelve-person black-robed chorus also sang Sands' music, which apparently resonated more powerfully (if sometimes too powerfully) in an intimate amphitheater ten feet in diameter with seating on both sides. Critics found the performances, especially that of Ann Mitchell as Hecuba, compelling. Mitchell's dignified, intelligent, and forceful restraint in this case enhanced her power. The emotional opening scenes were presented with 'tight-lipped, beady-eyed control broken by rare convulsive outbursts.'[27] After the death of Polydorus, Hecuba tells Agamemnon, with a 'wheezy, half-crazed laugh,' 'I am dead. I feel nothing.' She greeted the raving Polymestor with 'disturbingly detached curiosity ... a little appraising smile on her lips.'[28] Despite her move from this 'emotionally depleted state' to 'unblinking ruthlessness' and near-psychosis,[29] this Hecuba apparently retained the audience's sympathy during her gradual self-destruction, perhaps in part because both Agamemnon and Odysseus remained markedly distanced from her corrosive suffering.

Finally, the year 2004 saw a burst of smaller productions of the play as well. A 2004 off-off Broadway performance by Friendly Fire Productions starring Kristin Linklater as Hecuba, directed by Alex Lippard, and translated by William Arrowsmith at a tiny basement theater of the Culture Project as part of a Hellenic Festival at the New York Public Library successfully put debate and political rhetoric about justice at the center of this performance.[30] A famous voice coach, Linklater's own nuanced and, in the views of critics, highly relevant exploration in this performance of debasement of language and democratic values was shared by her strong male opponents. The audience, placed on either side of the debaters as in the Gate Theatre production, followed their verbal thrusts like a ping-pong match. Critic Gwen Orel went so far as to acclaim Linklater as a new Sarah Bernhardt.[31] If this production invited attention to tragic debate, the Foursight Theatre, an all-female British theater company representing various ethnic and linguistic origins, toured their production in 2004 to a wide range of audiences including schools and colleges. The production integrated voice, body, music, and movement, and used puppets for the children. Hecuba's shift from controlled to vengeful was the production's pivotal moment.[32] The play was directed by Naomi Cooke, with a translation by John Harrison; the six performers went in and out of the chorus.

In California, Workshop 360 in Los Angeles also offered a spare, postmodern performance starring Diana Castle in 2004 directed by L. Zane and translated by Timberlake Wertenbaker[33] and The Sixth at Penn Theater in San Diego staged Marianne McDonald's new translation directed by Esther Emery.[34] The 92nd Street Y in New York, gave a staged reading in 2004 of Anne Carson's new translation starring and directed by Kathryn Walker.[35] Finally, a new version, *The Memory of Salt*, was directed at the Boston Center for the Arts in 2004 by John Ambrosino, with a script by Liza Maurizio. This version featured Japanese-style music by Sachi Sato and a chorus of Salt Maidens who mined salt from water and haunted an Odysseus who learned to be sympathetic to Hecuba.[36] All of these 2004–5 productions explicitly responded to the Iraq War.

This discussion regrettably neglects important productions at other dates and in other languages—Greece, Germany and the Netherlands in particular have produced some recent outstanding versions—to say nothing of others in English (including Canada and Scotland as well as England and the US and excellent university productions) ranging from the 1950s to 2010. The Greek productions are simply too numerous to include here. Perhaps the most famous of these, which starred Katina Paxinou and was directed by Alexis Minotis, was performed from 1955–67 in Epidauros, Athens, Dodona, London, Bucharest, Zagreb, and Sofia. Nevertheless, the productions in English considered here contributed to the critical debate over the play by representing in performance virtually all the different perspectives adopted in the scholarly debate over the play and won a new level of recognition for the play itself.[37]

Chronology

BCE

Eighth–sixth centuries:	Texts of Homer's *Iliad* and *Odyssey* first written down.
Seventh–sixth centuries and later:	Epic cycle poems *Iliupersis*, *Cypria*, *Nostoi*.
Sixth century:	Stesichorus and Ibycus.
Sixth–fifth centuries:	Simonides.
Fifth century:	Herodotus and Thucydides.
Fifth–fourth centuries:	Lysias.
Fourth century:	Demosthenes.
c. 480:	Birth of Euripides.
472:	Aeschylus' *Persians*.
458:	Aeschylus' *Oresteia* (*Agamemnon*, *Libation Bearers*, *Eumenides*).
455:	Euripides' first production.
c. 447:	Sophocles' *Ajax*.
441:	Euripides' first victory.
c. 440–1:	Sophocles' *Antigone*.
438:	Euripides' *Alcestis*.
c. 430–28:	Euripides' *Children of Heracles*.
c. 429:	Sophocles' *Oedipus Tyrannus*.
431:	Outbreak of the Peloponnesian War between Athens and Sparta.
431:	Euripides' *Medea*.
428:	Euripides' *Hippolytus*.
427:	Mytilenean debate in the Athenian Assembly and revolution in Corcyra.
c. 425:	Euripides' *Andromache*.

424:	Battle of Delium in which Athens was ultimately defeated by Boeotia.
424–3:	Probable date of Euripides' *Hecuba*.
c. 424–20:	Euripides' *Suppliant Women*.
c. 423:	Euripides' *Erectheus*.
423:	Aristophanes' *Clouds* (first version).
422–15:	Euripides' *Heracles*.
415:	Euripides' *Trojan Women* (with *Alexander*, *Palamedes* and the satyr play *Sisyphus*).
c. 418–10:	Sophocles' *Electra*.
c. 414–12:	Euripides' *Ion*.
c. 413:	Euripides' *Electra*.
411:	Oligarchic Regime of the Four Hundred at Athens.
c. 409:	Euripides' *Phoenician Women*.
408:	Euripides' *Orestes*.
408/7:	Euripides goes to Macedonia.
407/6:	Euripides dies in Macedonia.
After 406:	Euripides' *Bacchae* and *Iphigenia at Aulis* produced in Athens.
404:	Athens defeated by Sparta in the Peloponnesian War.
386:	Regular revivals of Greek tragedy introduced at the City Dionysia.
c. 330:	Aristotle's *Poetics*.
Second century:	Ennius, Pacuvius.
First century:	Catullus, poem 64.
29–19:	Vergil, *Aeneid*.

CE

8:	Ovid, *Metamorphoses*.
mid-first century:	Seneca, *Troades*.
Second century:	Plutarch and Pausanias.

Fourth century:	Quintus of Smyrnaeus and Dictys of Crete.
1506:	Desiderius Erasmus' Latin translation of *Hecuba* and *Iphigenia Among the Taurians* based on the 1503 edition of Marcus Musurus.
1506–14:	Production of *Hecuba* by Melanchthon, Collège du Porc, Belgium.
1525:	Production of *Hecuba* by Melanchton, Wittenberg, Germany.
1562:	First Greek–Latin edition of Euripides' works by Gasparus Stiblinus.
1579:	*La Troade*, adaptation of *Hecuba*, *Trojan Women* and Seneca's *Troades*, France.
1594:	*Polyxène*, France.
1707:	*Le Rovine di Troia*, Italian opera version, based on *Hecuba*, *Trojan Women* and Seneca's *Troades*, Teatro S. Cassiano, Venice.
1715:	*Polidoro*, opera based on Euripides' *Andromache* and *Hecuba*, by Antonio Lotti, Venice.
1726:	*Hecuba*, blank-verse translation by Richard West, Drury Lane, London, with Mary Ann Porter as Hecuba.
1736:	*Hekuba*, revised as *Troianerinnen*, based on *Hecuba*, *Trojan Women* and Seneca's *Troades* by Johann Elias Schlegel, Germany.
1761:	*Hecuba*, adaptation by John Delap, Drury Lane, London, with Mrs Pritchard as Hecuba.
1782:	*Troianerinnen*, based on *Hecuba*, *Trojan Women*, and Seneca's *Troades* by Johann Elias Schlegel, Burgtheater, Vienna.
1792:	*Hécube*, version at the Comédie Française, Paris.
1793:	*Hécube*, translation at the Théâtre de la Nation, Paris.

1800:	*Hécube*, French opera version by Granges de Fontenelle, Théâtre des Arts, Paris.
1817:	*Ekavi*, Academy of Ayvalik, Istanbul, Turkey.
1817:	*Ekavi*, Company of Rallou Karatza, Greece, Bucharest, Romania.
1827:	*Hecuba*, directed by Richard Valpy in Greek at the Reading Town Hall, Reading, England.
1856:	*Ekavi*, Hellenoemporiki Scholi, Chalki, Greece performed by students at a carnival.
1866:	*Ekavi*, Naoum Theatre, Istanbul.
1867:	*Ekavi*, Gymnasio Peiraios, Greece.
1887:	*Ekavi*, by Menandros company, Greece.
1893:	*Hecuba à la mode: or The Wily Greek and the Modest Maid*, burlesque by Cranstoun Metcalfe, London.
1896:	*Ekavi*, Thiasos Aristofanis of Dimitris Kotopoulis, Greece.
1916:	*Hekabe*, Teatr Miejski, Jagiellonian University, Krakow, Poland, translated Boguslaw Butymowicz.
1927–28:	*Ekavi*, Company of Marika Kotopouli, directed by Fotos Politis, Ancient Stadium of Athens, Demotiko Theatro, Piraeus, and Theatro Louna Park, Greece.
1938:	*The Bride of a Ghost* or *Polyxena*, a new version by Henry Bertram Lister for the La Bohème Club of San Francisco.
1939:	*Ecuba*, Istituto Nazionale del Dramma Antico, Siracusa, Italy, directed by Vincenzo Bonaiuto.
1943:	*Ekavi*, Ethniko Theatro (National Theatre of Greece), translated by Nikos Poriotis, directed by Sokratis Karantinos.

1947:	*Hecuba*, Randolph Macon Woman's College, Ashland, Virginia, directed by Mabel K. Whiteside.
1949:	*The House of Atreus*, a trilogy of abridged adaptations of *Hecuba*, Aeschylus' *Agamemnon*, and Sophocles' *Electra* by Burton Crane, Exchange Hotel Theatre, Tokyo Amateur Dramatic Club, Tokyo.
1952:	*Ekavi*, Pagkyprion Gymnasium, Nicosia, Cyprus, directed by Th. Sophokleous.
1955–67:	*Ekavi*, directed by Alexis Minotis, starring Katina Paxinou, performed in Epidauros, Athens, Dodona, London, Bucharest, Zagreb and Sofia.
1962:	*Ecuba*, Istituto Nazionale del Dramma Antico, Siracusa, Italy, translated by Salvatore Quasimodo, directed by Giuseppe Di Martino.
1962:	*Ekavi*, Hellenikon Gymnasium Pafou, Paphos, Cyprus, directed by Aris Georgiou and Nikos Hellinas.
1963:	*Ecuba*, directed Enrico d'Alessandro, Teatro dei Convegno, Milan, Italy.
1967:	*Cortege of Eagles*, Martha Graham's dance version of *Trojan Women* and *Hecuba*, settings by Isamu Noguchi, lighting by Jean Rosenthal, music by Eugene Lester, starring Graham as Hecuba, later performed a number of times in New York.
1967:	*Hecuba* by Jack Lindsay, performed with *Iphigenia in Aulis*, *Electra*, and *Orestes* as *The Trojan Wars*, Mermaid Theatre, London, England.
1979:	*Hecuba*, adapted and directed by Branko Plesa in Serbia and Montenegro.

1979:	*Hecuba*, Winged Horse Productions, Traverse Theatre, Edinburgh, Scotland, composed by John Sampson, script by Stewart Conn.
1981:	*Ekavi*, Imikratiko Theatro Peloponnisou, directed by Nikos Perelis, Peloponnese, Greece.
1981:	*Ekavi*, Company of Dimitris Myrat and Voula Zoumboulaki, directed by Dimitris Myrat, Odeon Herodes Atticus, Athens, Greece.
1981:	*Ekavi*, State Theatre of Northern Greece, directed by Leonidas Trivizas at Philippi, Thasos, Thessaloniki, and Epidaurus, Greece and Mexico.
1983:	*Ekavi*, Desmoi Cultural and Artistic Association, directed by Heinz-Uwe Haus, Lycabettus Theatre, Athens, Greece.
1984:	*The Lost Women of Troy*, Cameri Theatre, Israel, directed by Hanoch Levin.
1985:	*Ekavi*, National Theatre of Greece, directed by Lambros Kostopoulos, Athens and Epidauros, Greece.
1986:	*Ekavi*, Lykeio Ethn. Makariou-Paphou, Ancient Odeon of Paphos, Cyprus.
1987:	*Hecuba*, Manara Productions, directed by Lamis Khalaf, Powerhouse Theater in Santa Monica, California, starring Susan Nazami as Hecuba.
1987:	*Ekavi*, Proskino Company of Alexis Solomos, directed by Alexis Solomos, music by Mikis Theodorakis, Epidauros and Lycabettus Theater, Athens.
1987:	*Hecuba*, Qwirk Productions, New York.
1988:	*Ekavi*, Theatrikos Organismos Kyprou (THOK), Cyprus, directed by Nikos Charalambous. Epidauros, Greece.

1988:	*L'Hécube*, translation by Nicole Loraux and François Rey, directed Bernard Sobel, Théâtre du Gennevilliers, Paris, France.
1989–90:	*Ekave*, Shoestring, directed Dennis Douglas, Clarendon Press Institute, Oxford, England.
1989:	*Hecuba*, Winged Horse Productions, directed John Carnegie, Scotland.
1991:	*Hecuba*, directed Emilio Hernández, Ancient Theatre of Mérida, Teatro Romano, Extramadura, Spain.
1991:	*Hekuba*, directed by Ivica Boban, Gradac Park, Dubrovnik, Croatia.
1992:	*Hecuba*, Gate Theatre, London, translated by Kenneth McLeish, directed by Laurence Boswell, starring Ann Mitchell as Hecuba.
1993:	*Hekabe*, Actors of Dionysus, translated and directed by David Stuttard, England.
1993:	*Hecuba*, Theatre Carleton, Canada, directed by Douglas Campbell.
1995:	*Hécuba*, Théâtre à Dire, directed by Alain Michel, France.
1995 and 1998:	*Hekabe*, American Conservatory Theater, San Francisco at the Yerba Buena Center in 1995 and 1998 at the Geary Theatre and the Theatre Festival in Williamstown, Massachusetts, directed by Carey Perloff, starring Olympia Dukakis as Hekabe.
1995:	*Hekabe*, RO Theater, translated by Gerard Koolschijn, directed by Peter de Baan, Rotterdam, Arnheim, and Eindhoven, North Brabant, Netherlands.

1996: *The Greeks: Trojan Women* (adapted by Keith Cavendish) and *Hecuba* (adapted by John Barton), St Louis Shakespeare Company, Grandel Square Theater, St Louis, directed by Donna Northcott, starring Teresa Dogget as Hecuba.

1996: *Hecuba*, Unseame'd Shakespeare Company, Luciano's Coffee House, Pittsburgh, translated by Joel Tanseu and Kiki Gounaridou, directed Tim Golebiewski, with Rebekah Slotnick as Hecuba.

1996: *Hecuba*, University of Oxford, Oxford University Classical Drama Society, David Raeburn.

1997: *Hekabe*, Classical Drama Group, Trent University, Peterborough, Ontario, Canada, directed by Martin Boyne.

1997: *Hécuba*, Grupo Teatro Experimental de Tebas, Greece, performed in the Ancient Theater of Segóbriga, Spain.

1998: *Ecuba*, Istituto Nazionale del Dramma Antico, Siracusa, Italy, directed by Lorenzo Salveti.

1998: *Hecuba*, The African Continuum Theater Company's (ACTCo) Living Stage, Washington, DC, directed by Jennifer Nelson, translation by Marilyn Nelson, starring Cheryl Collins as Hecuba.

1999: *Hekabe*, translated by Michael Wachsmann, directed by Dieter Dorn, Münchner Kammerspiele Schauspielhaus, Munich, starring Gisela Stein as Hekabe.

1999:	*Hecuba*, Cypresco Theater Group, Queens Borough Public Library and other Queens sites, New York City.
2000:	*Hecuba*, Barnard College, Columbia University, New York, directed in Greek by Devon Harlow.
2000:	*Hekabe*, directed by Christoph Schroth, Staatstheater, Cottbus, Brandenburg, Germany.
2000:	*Hekabe*, Puppentheater, Dresden, Germany.
2001:	*Ekavi*, Teatro Stoa, directed by Thanasis Papageorgiou, Athens, Greece.
2001:	*Ekavi*, State Theatre of Northern Greece, directed by Diagoras Chronopoulos, Epidauros, Greece.
2002:	*Ecuba*, new opera by Bruno Rigacci, Brooklyn College Conservatory Orchestra, Brooklyn, New York, directed by Mignon Dunn.
2003:	*Hekabe*, Theater am Kirchpatz, Liechtenstein, directed by Wolfgang Heyder.
2003:	*Hecuba*, Amphi-Theatro of Spyros Evangelatos, directed by Spyros Evangelatos, Epidauros, Greece.
2003:	*Hecuba, Bitch of Cynossema*, Teatro Technis, London, England.
2004:	*Hecuba*, a version by Frank McGuinness based on a literal translation by Fionnuala Murphy, Donmar Warehouse, London, directed by Jonathan Kent, starring Clare Higgins as Hecuba.
2004:	*Hecuba*, Foursight Theatre touring production in the West Midlands, England, translated by John Harrison, and directed by Naomi Cooke.

2004:	*Hecuba*, Workshop 360, Los Angeles, California, translated by Timberlake Wertenbaker, directed by L. Zane, and starring Diana Castle.
2004:	*Hecuba*, sixth at Penn Theater, San Diego, translated by Marianne McDonald, directed by Esther Emery.
2004:	*Hecuba*, 92nd Street Y, New York, a staged reading of Anne Carson's translation directed by and starring Kathryn Walker.
2004:	*The Memory of Salt*, directed by John Ambrosino with a script by Liza Maurizio, Boston Center for the Arts, Boston.
2004:	*Hecuba*, Friendly Fire Productions, translated by William Arrowsmith, directed by Alex Lippard, starring Kristin Linklater as Hecuba, Culture Project, New York.
2005:	*Hecuba*, Royal Shakespeare Company, Albery Theatre, London, translated by Tony Harrison, directed by Laurence Boswell, starring Vanessa Redgrave; directed by Tony Harrison, Brooklyn Academy of Music, New York, and Kennedy Center, Washington, DC, and Delphi, Greece.
2005:	*Hecuba*, Academy Drama School, London, directed by Tim Barron.
2006:	*Ecuba*, Istituto del Dramma Antico, composed by Arturo Annecchino, translated by Umberto Albini with Assistant director, Maro Plini, Siracusa, Italy.
2006:	*Hecuba*, Pearl Theater, New York City, directed by Shepard Sobel, starring Joanne Camp as Hecuba.

2007:	*Hekabe*, New York University, Experimental Theater Wing, Frederick Lowe Theater, directed by Magdalena Zira, New York.
2009:	*Hecuba*, Theater for the New City, New York, directed by Joan Kane.
2010:	*Blind Eye Crying*, *Hecuba* and *Trojan Women*, Lifeblood Theatre Company, Oxford, Onassis Programme, directed by Alex Clifton, called *After Troy* in 2011, Oxford Playhouse, Oxford and Shaw Theatre, London.
2010:	*Hecuba*, New Diorama Theatre, directed by Ricky Dukes, London.
Note:	This list of performances eliminates most university productions, and others that are less documented or very loosely related to Euripides' *Hecuba*. For further detail, see The Archive of Performances of Greek and Roman Drama (APGRD).

Glossary of Ancient and Technical Terms

Aeolo-choriambic meter: an elaborate lyric meter that embeds a unit of one long syllable, two short syllables, and another long syllable (-uu-) in longer lines of sung verse.

Agalma: monument or statue.

Agôn: a formal debate (or 'contest') scene between two dramatic characters.

Alastôr: a personified power of vengeance for spilled blood (Burkert 1985, 184).

Anapestic meter: a metrical unit consisting of two short syllables and one long syllable (uu-) that usually occurs in pairs. When used in recitative it often accompanies walking or marching; lyric anapests are sung to a melody and more flexible.

Aretê: virtue, functional excellence.

Aulos: double pipe played to accompany choral music and dance in drama.

Charis: gratitude, reciprocity, kindness, sexual favor.

Chitôn: a rectangle of wool or linen worn as a garment (in this play by women) fastened at the shoulders.

Chorêgos: a wealthy citizen chosen to produce one poet's sets of three tragedies and a satyr play and train its chorus.

Dactylo-epitrite meter: a high-style lyric meter that combines the dactylic meter of epic (six units with one long syllable followed by two short syllables or two longs, -uu or --) with iambic and aeolo-choriambic rhythms.

Dikê: justice, lawsuit, punishment (**dikên didonai** means to pay a penalty).

Dithyramb: choral song performed in competition by ten groups of fifty men and fifty boys at the Athenian City Dionysia or festival in honor of the theater god Dionysus.

Dochmiac meter: a lyric meter exclusive to drama that is restricted to moments of high emotion.

Eikos: an argument from *eikos* is an argument from probability.
Ekkyklêma: a wheeled platform that could be rolled out from within the **skênê**, commonly used in tragedy to show a scene taking place inside and especially to display dead bodies.
Episode: scene of a tragedy.
Erôs: erotic desire.
Geras: prize.
Iambic trimeter: the meter used for speeches and dialog in tragedy. The basic rhythmic pattern is x-u-x-u-x-u- where - is a long syllable, u is a short syllable, and x can be short or long syllable or two short syllables.
Mêchanê: a crane used to swing actors, usually divinities, above the stage building.
Monody: an actor's solo song.
Nomos: law, custom, convention.
Orchêstra: a 'dancing space' for the chorus between the audience and the stage building (*skênê*).
Parodoi or **Eisodoi**: paths from both sides of the **skênê** leading into the orchestra that were used for entrances to and from the city or location where the tragedy is set. **Parodos** is also used for the entrance song of the chorus.
Peithô: persuasion.
Peplos: a long tubular robe folded over at the top, gathered at the waist, and pinned at the shoulders.
Philos: friend, relative. **Philia** means friendship or alliance.
Polis: city-state.
Praxis: tragic action.
Protagonist: the first actor in a group of three who performed all the roles in a Greek tragedy.
Scholion: an ancient note written on the margins of a papyrus or medieval manuscript.
Skênê: wooden stage building with a central door.
Sophisma: sophism, captious argument.
Stasimon: choral ode sung between episodes (after the entrance song or **parodos**) that is divided into pairs of metrically

equivalent stanzas (*strophe* and *antistrophe*); an additional stanza called an *epode* can be added after strophic pairs.
Timôria: revenge.
Tyrannos: ruler, sovereign.
Xenia: guest friendship, hospitality (a **xenos** is a host or guest).

Guide to Further Reading

Texts and Commentaries

Battezatto, L. *Euripide Ecuba*. Milano: BUR (Rizzoli), 2010. Greek text with an Italian translation and an extensive introduction.

Collard, C. *Euripides Hecuba*. Warminster: Aris and Phillips, 1991. Greek text, prose translation, introduction, and commentary with notes designed for both classicists and readers with limited Greek.

Daitz, S. J. *Euripides Hecuba*. Leipzig: B. G.Teubner, 1973, 1990. Edition of the Greek text with useful metrical appendices.

Diggle, J. *Euripidis Fabulae*, Vol. 1. Oxford: Oxford University Press, 1984. The standard edition of Euripides in the Oxford Classical Texts Series.

Gregory, J. *Euripides Hecuba. Introduction, Text, and Commentary*. Atlanta, GA: Scholar's Press, 1999. Edition of the Greek text, introduction, and commentary designed for students.

Kovacs, D. *Euripides*, Vol. 2. Cambridge, MA: Harvard University Press, 1995. Edition of the Greek text with prose translation for the Loeb Classical Library series.

Matthiessen, K. *Euripides Hekabe*. Berlin and New York: W. de Gruyter, 2008. Greek text with introduction and commentary in German.

Méridier, L. *Euripide*, Vol. 2. Paris: Les Belles Lettres, 1927. A critical edition of the Greek text with a French translation.

Perdicoyianni, H. *Commentaire sur l'Hécube d'Euripide*. Athens: Les Editions Historiques St.D. Basilopoulos, 1991. Recent short commentary in French.

Synodinou, K. *Euripides, Ekabe*. Athens: Daidalos-I. Zacharopoulos, 2005. Commentary in Greek.

Tierney, M. J. *Euripides Hecuba*. Dublin 1946: repr. Bristol: Bristol Classical Press 1981. Greek text with commentary for students.

Scholia

Schwartz, E. (ed.) *Scholia in Euripidem*, Vol. 1. Berlin: G. Reimer, 1891 and Berlin: W. de Gruyter, 1966.

English Translations without accompanying Greek text

(* has been successfully used for a staged production; all but one of these are discussed in 8. **Performances of *Hecuba***)

*Arrowsmith, W. In D. Grene and R. Lattimore (eds), *Euripides III, Hecuba, Andromache, Trojan Women, Ion*. Chicago, IL: University of Chicago Press, 1958. Verse translation.

*Carson, A. *Grief Lessons: Four Plays by Euripides*. New York: New York Review of Books, 2006.

*Harrison, T. *Hecuba by Euripides*. London: Faber and Faber, 2005. Originally designed for a staged production.

*Lembke, J. and K. Reckford. In Alan Shapiro and Peter Burian (eds), *Euripides Hecuba*. Oxford: Oxford University Press, 1991. A collective effort by a poet (Lembke) and a classicist (Reckford) with a provocative introduction and notes.

*McDonald, M. *Hecuba by Euripides*. London: Nick Hern Books, 2005. Originally designed for a staged production.

*McGuinness, F. *Hecuba in a new version by Frank McGuinness from a literal translation by Fionnuala Murphy*. London: Faber and Faber, 2004. Originally designed for a staged production.

*McLeish, K. *After the Trojan War: Women of Troy, Hecuba, Helene: Three Plays by Euripides*. Bath, England: Absolute Classics, 1995.

Mitchell-Boyask, R. *Odysseus at Troy: Sophocles' Ajax, and Euripides' Hecuba and Trojan Women*. Newbury Port, MA: Focus Publishers, 2010. Designed to be readily available for students.

Morwood, J. and E. Hall. *Trojan Women and Other Plays. Hecuba, Trojan Women, Andromache*. Oxford: Oxford University Press

(Oxford World Classics), 2001. Available translation by Morwood with introduction by Hall.
*Nelson, M. *Hecuba.* In D. Slavitt and P. Bowie (eds), *Euripides 1: Medea, Hecuba, Andromache, Bacchae.* Philadelphia, PA: University of Pennsylvania Press, 1997.
*Wertenbaker, T. *Euripides' Hecuba.* Woodstock, IL; London, England; Melbourne, Australia: Dramatic Publishing, 1995. Originally designed for a staged production.

Selected Secondary Reading on *Hecuba*

Gregory, J. *Euripides and the Instruction of the Athenians.* Ann Arbor, MI: University of Michigan Press, 1991. Chapter on *Hecuba* usefully contextualizes the play in its political context.

Heath, M. '*Jure principen locum tenet.* Euripides' *Hecuba,*' *Bulletin of the Institute of Classical Studies* 34, 40–68 (1987a). An important article on the reception of *Hecuba.*

Kastely, J. L. 'Rhetoric and Violence in Euripides' *Hecuba,*' *Proceedings of the Modern Language Association* 108, no. 5: 1036–49 (1993). Interesting literary study that emphasizes the role of rhetoric in the play.

Kovacs, D. *The Heroic Muse. Studies in the Hippolytus and Hecuba of Euripides.* Baltimore, MD: Johns Hopkins University Press, 1987. Chapter on *Hecuba* contests negative readings of the play and Hecuba's character.

Michelini, A. *Euripides and the Tragic Paradox.* Madison, WI: University of Wisconsin Press, 1987. Chapter on *Hecuba* argues for Hecuba's moral and rhetorical decline in the play.

Mossman, J. *Wild Justice: A Study of Euripides' Hecuba.* Oxford: Oxford University Press, 1995. Comprehensive study of the play and its reception.

Zeitlin, F. I. 'Euripides' *Hekabe* and the Somatics of Dionysiac Drama,' *Ramus* 20, no. 1: 53–94 (1991); revised in 1996 in her *Playing the Other: Gender and Society in Classical Greek Literature,* 172–218.

Chicago, IL: University of Chicago Press. Provocative discussion of major themes in the play.

General Studies on Euripides in English

Conacher, D. J. *Euripidean Drama: Myth, Theme, and Structure.* Toronto: University of Toronto Press, 1967. Older literary introduction to all of Euripides' plays.

Mastronarde, D. *The Art of Euripides: Dramatic Technique and Social Context.* Cambridge: Cambridge University Press, 2010. Recent study of Euripides' dramatic techniques.

Notes

Chapter 1

1 For a discussion of the play's probable extensive influence on *Hamlet*, see Pollard 2012.
2 The parody of Euripides' monodies at Aristophanes' *Frogs* 1331–7 may refer to Hecuba's opening black-winged dream (71, 705). Euripidean plays often had female protagonists narrate frightening dreams to the open air at the beginning of his plays. *Hecuba* was quoted later in Antiquity by authors such as Strabo, Lucian, Hermogenes, and Libanius (Heath 1987a, 42).
3 Evidence for actor's interpolations in the text of *Hecuba* also suggests re-performances of the play in the fourth century BCE and later (Heath 1987a, 41).
4 Montanari 1987, 27–8 cites eleven such papyri from 200 BCE to 250 CE. There are seventeen papyri from the even more popular *Phoenician Women* and thirteen from *Orestes*. There were three hundred medieval and renaissance manuscripts of *Hecuba* from 1000 to 1600 CE. See Matthiessen 1974 for the history of the text.
5 Heath 1987a, 43 and, more generally, Cribiore 2001. In *Orestes*, the hero has just killed his mother Clytemnestra to avenge her murder of his father Agamemnon, and later tries and fails to avenge himself on Helen. In *Phoenician Women* the angry brothers Eteocles and Polyneices fail to resolve their conflicts over ruling Thebes and decide to meet in a fatal duel.
6 Translated Palima 2002.
7 See Loraux 1986.
8 Herman 1987.
9 All translations of Thucydides are by J. H. Finley, Jr. 1951.
10 Gregory 1991, 100, 113. She argues (85) that the play responds to Athenian imperialism and the relations between powerful and

powerless that developed during this period. Fear, honor, and advantage compel the Athenians to retain their empire in Thucydides (1.75.3) and also motivate the Greek generals in *Hecuba*. For further relevant historical examples, see Hogan 1972.
11 Herman 1987.
12 Segal 1993, 210 defines the world of the play as one that 'has lost touch with basic moral values and with a language that could articulate them.' On the relativizing of moral terminology in the play, he adds (211), 'in *Hecuba*, Euripides holds out the possibility of universal moral laws, but he also shows us a world not ready for them.'
13 Segal 1993, 211. Recourse to self-help justice in reality was rare in Athens (see especially Cohen 1995 and Herman 1994 and 1995).
14 See, for example, Aeschylus, *Agamemnon* 485–6 on the dangers of female credulity and persuasion. The democracy grew increasingly hostile to public interventions by aristocratic women like Cimon's half-sister Elpinice (Plutarch, *Pericles* 28).
15 See e.g. Plutarch, *Solon* 21.2–3 on invalidating wills influenced by 'the persuasion of a woman/wife,' and the role of female persuasion in a similar court case, Demosthenes 6.48. For further discussion, see Foley 2001, 273–6.
16 See especially Foley 2001, 19–55 with further bibliography and Billing 2007.

Chapter 2

1 The number depends on the size of the theater in the fifth century. On the controversy, see Csapo 2000 and Wiles 1997. For sources on the Greek theater, see Csapo and Slater 1995.
2 Henderson 1991; Goldhill 1994; Roselli 2011, 154–67, 186–94, 199–200.

3 Goldhill 1987.
4 See note 1.
5 Mossman 1995, 49.
6 Collard 1991a, 36.
7 I follow Collard 1991a, 37 here.
8 Burnett 1998, 158–61 stresses that once the chorus has entered, women dominate the stage in numbers, unity, and ability to sympathize with each other and to cross cultural boundaries in their imagination.
9 See Seaford 1982; Zeitlin 1991; Cropp and Fick 1985.
10 Collard 1991a, 135.
11 My translation.
12 On Sophocles' play, see Mossman 1995, 42–6 and Gregory 1999, xv.
13 King 1985, especially 48, 50–4. On the sources for this episode, see Conacher 1961, 3–7 and Mossman 1995, chapter 1.
14 For further discussion of this and other images not discussed here, see Mossman 1995, 256–1 and the entries on Hecuba and Polyxena in LIMC (*Lexicon Iconographicum Mythologiae Classicae*).
15 Sevinç 1996; Durand and Lissarrague 1999, 97–8; Neer 2012; Holzman 2012; Rose 2013, 72–103. The sarcophagus contained the body of a forty-year old man, but it may have been designed for a woman (Rose 2013, 95–8).
16 This image may have been inspired by representations of Achilles' falling in love with the Amazon Penthesileia at the moment he killed her.
17 Rose 2013, 82–3.
18 Some scholars have suggested that this is a wedding scene, perhaps even that of Neoptolemus and Andromache. The broader Anatolian context suggests a somewhat unusual funerary context (Rose 2013, 91–5).
19 Rose 2013, 90 and n. 91 notes that Achilles performed a pyrrhic dance at Patroclus' tomb in the *Iliad* and that Neoptolemus may have invented the pyrrhic dance.

20 The Ilioupersis cup by the Brygos Painter (early fifth century BCE, Louvre G 152) shows Polyxena, led by Athamas and looking back at Neoptolemus attacking a seated Priam with the body of Astyanax. An Etruscan mirror at the Musée des Beaux-Arts in Lyon dated third century BCE shows a nude Polyxena lying on Hecuba's lap with two nude warriors surrounding them. See also Rose 2013, 302, n. 55.

21 Fontinoy 1955, Conacher 1961, 3, and Mossman 1995, 247–53 discuss post-Hellenistic versions that romanticize the relation between Achilles and Polyxena. See especially, Vergil, *Aeneid* 3.321, Catullus 64, 367–70, Dictys of Crete 3.2–3, 5, 24; 4.11, Seneca, *Troades*, Quintus Smyrnaeus, *Posthomerica*, Ennius, *Hecuba* and Pacuvius, *Ilione*.

22 In Euripides' later play *Iphigenia in Aulis* Iphigenia is enticed to Aulis by the promise of betrothal to Achilles.

23 Thalmann 1993, 155, asks whether, if the entire action is framed by the sacrifice of an innocent girl, has anything changed, or is change possible?

24 King 1985; Thalmann 1993.

25 The Polydorus story might be derived from *Iliad* 19, 326–27 where we are told that Achilles' son Neoptolemus has been left in Skyros in order to protect his life.

26 For later artistic representations of Hecuba herself, see Mossman 1995, 254–56.

27 Mossman 1995, 39–41.

28 Burnett 1994, 161; Mossman 1995, 34. In later sources like Nikander of Colophon (scholion at *Hecuba* 3) she turns into a dog at Troy and dashes into the sea (second century BCE). Lykophron 330–4, 1174–88 has her turned into a dog and stoned; she goes to Hades and becomes a hound of Hekate (third century BCE). In Quintus Smyrnaeus 14.347–91 the gods turn her into a dog, then into stone; Dictys of Crete 5.16 (fourth century CE) omits her transformation into a dog, but has her stoned to death after cursing the Greeks and buried at Cynossema. See further Gantz 1993, 660.

29 Zeitlin 1991, 54 also notes that the play links past and future.
30 Hall 1989, 109 expanding on Delebecque 1951, 147–64.
31 Hall 1989, 110.

Chapter 3

1 Tetsall 1954.
2 My translation.
3 Translations of *Hecuba* from 714–15 on are from Collard 1991a.
4 See Collard 1991a, 176 and Gregory 1999, 161.
5 Among some earlier critics, Pohlenz 1954, 281 saw the play as unified by the changing figure of Hecuba, Kirkwood 1947 thought the play focused on the theme of *nomos* (law, convention), and Fitzgerald 1989, 221 found the play unified by the child murder theme (see also Tarkow 1984).
6 Kastely 1993, 1036.
7 Michelini 1987, 141–3, views Hecuba's rhetoric as deceptive, self-destructive, and self-betraying as well as designed to sting, not convince. See also Matthaei 1918, 148; Buxton 1982, 184; Segal 1993, 208; Rabinowitz 1993, 113.
8 Reckford 1985 effectively summarizes the case for Hecuba's negative evolution and dehumanization in a demoralized world. Abrahamson 1952, 121 called *Hecuba* 'a concentration camp play.' Other critics who take this position include Matthaei 1918; Kirkwood 1947, 66–7; Conacher 1961, 18–19, 23, 26; 1967, 160–3; Hogan 1972; Luschnig 1976, 230–1; Buxton 1982, 180, 181; Nussbaum 1986, 415–16; Michelini 1987; Segal 1993, especially 158; Rabinowitz 1993, 121; Burnett 1998, 167. Conacher 1961, 25 allows Hecuba a tragic decline not a tragic peripety (reversal of fortune).
9 In Reckford's view (1985, 124) she is brought to the level of her oppressors and to spiritual slavery.
10 Kastely 1993, 1036–7. Michelini 1987, 157 argues that in this play moral norms have no force as long as political goals are in question.

11 Kastely 1993, 1039, whose views in many respects overlap with those of Gregory 1991.
12 Kastely 1993, 1041.
13 Kastely 1993, 1047.
14 Mossman 1995, 209. Collard 1991a, 28 stresses the constant reference to language and its powers in the play.
15 See Mossman 1995, 102 and Gregory 1999, xxxiii on Hecuba's stable character. Kovacs 1987, 99 finds no moral decline. Gregory emphasizes that even though numb to her own fate, Hecuba continues to care for her children until the end of the play.
16 Buxton 1982, 177.
17 Gregory 1991, 108.
18 Meridor 1983, 15, citing MacDowell 1978, 79–83. Agamemnon should in principle act for his wronged slave (Meridor, 15–16). Meridor also stresses that Athens prided itself on its humane treatment of slaves. See Mossman 1995, 180, n. 81 on women as appropriate avengers in the absence of male relatives to do so.
19 Kovacs 1987, 80–81, 99 sees Hecuba as adhering to a consistent code of traditional morality that belongs to a vanished world in the face of secular, unprincipled Greeks. This code includes avenging injuries. See Mossman 1995, 171–2 on the dangers of unavenged victims in Greek myth and culture.
20 For an excellent discussion of the language used for revenge, punishment, and justice in both the play and the larger cultural context, see Battezatto 2010, 13–59.
21 Meridor 1978 and 1983; Mossman 1995, 4, 164–5. Others who resist the view that Hecuba's revenge is a sign of degeneration, include Gregory 1991 and 1999, xxxiii; Kovacs 1987; Gellie 1980; Erbse 1984; Steidle 1966; Schlesier 1988; Zeitlin 1991. Kitto 1961, 222 views both sides as wrongdoers and victims; Thalmann 1993, 149 and Battezatto 2010 view the outcome as more ambivalent.
22 Zeitlin 1991, 56; Segal 1993, 174 also remarks on the common reversal of tragic women from victim to agent of violence. Rabinowitz 1993, 123–4 argues that the plays incorporate women into the male meaning machine and ultimately silence them.

23 See further below.
24 On rhetoric and characterization in tragedy, see Mossman 1995, 94–102.
25 Michelini 1987, 134–5.
26 Zeitlin 1991, 80–3. As she stresses, touch and pity are intimately linked in the play.
27 Zeitlin 1991, 65. On the role of the gaze in this play, see also Zeitlin 64–7, 90, n. 40.
28 Gregory 1991, especially 85.

Chapter 4

1 For this scene, see Jouanna 1982.
2 Jouanna 1982 and most others think he appears on the *skênê* roof; Lane 2007 argues for Polydorus on stage level with Hecuba lying on the ground before him.
3 Zeitlin 1991, 53.
4 Battezatto 2010, 9, 78.
5 Hall 2006, 313.
6 On the question of whether or not Achilles specifically demanded Polyxena, a Trojan woman, or simply a *geras* or prize, see especially Gregory 1999, xxiv–xxxix. The text is inconsistent on this point, but Polydorus' opening speech would in my view have established Polyxena as the victim; we cannot interpret his words as referring only to what eventually happens.
7 The *Iliad* turns on the question of who is 'the best of the Achaeans', Achilles or Agamemnon.
8 See Gregory 1999, xxix–xxxi on the role of wind in the play discussed further below.
9 See Collard 1991a, 139 on the matching lyrics here.
10 Zeitlin 1991, 55.
11 Lloyd 1992, 8–9 refuses to categorize this scene as a tragic debate because the speeches are not followed by contentious dialog, but

Mossman 1995, 55 and Collard 1991a, 143 rightly do so. On the structure of the *agôn* speech, see Collard 1991a, 145.
12 Conacher 1961, 16–17 emphasizes Hecuba's outstanding rhetorical skill.
13 Mossman 1995, 105, 113.
14 Mercier 1990. Hecuba mentions her supplication of Odysseus at 273 and 286. It is unclear when she stops supplicating (see Mossman 1995, 56; Gregory 1999, 86). Heath 1987b, 146 argues that no actual supplication takes place.
15 If it is not appropriate to sacrifice humans, it is in principle also questionable to sacrifice Helen. Hecuba's speech is contradictory on this point, even if Helen lacks Polyxena's innocence.
16 Conacher 1961, 12; Synodinou 1994–5, 191–3, and Abrahamson 1952, 124 offer some of the most forceful questions about Odysseus' speech. Synodinou questions the argument of Matthaei 1918, who saw the debate as a clash between individual and collective interests. For Vellacott 1975, 208 the question is not whether Achilles is entitled to honor, but to what honor he is entitled. In Conacher's view (1961, 5), political expediency plays a more important role in Odysseus' argument than religious necessity. For further questions about Odysseus' argument, see O'Connor-Visser 1987, 63, 67.
17 Kovacs 1987, 89 and Buxton 1982, 174 note Odysseus' merely instrumental view of morality. For him, all necessity is political (Buxton, 177). See Adkins 1966, 198–9 for the traditional basis of claims concerning *aretê* (virtue) and *philia* in Odysseus' argument; Hogan 1972, 241–2 thinks Adkins over-simplifies the moral conflict in this scene by removing all authority from Hecuba's position. See also Michelini 1987, 146, who supports Adkins, and Thalmann 1993, 138.
18 Kastely 1993, 1037; Abrahamson 1952, 123–4, n.10; Conacher 1967, 157–8.
19 Matthaei 1918 influentially argued that the entire play pits the formal or social justice of the community against personal, instinctive, or 'natural' justice represented by the relatively weak

arguments offered by Hecuba. The play thus pits the individual against the community.
20 Kovacs 1987, 82–3.
21 Kastely 1993, 1038.
22 On her speech, see Collard 1991a, 158 and Pagani 1970, 56–60.
23 Mossman 1995, 57.
24 If her fear is plausible, Hecuba interprets Polyxena's gesture as inviting a sexual response.
25 On this speech, see Mossman 1995, 120–2 and Gregory 1999, 117–19.
26 Kastley 1993, 1039 argues that Polyxena's death allows the brutality of those in power; the suffering of war continues; and noble birth and being above circumstance has become meaningless. Mitchell-Boyask 1993, 121–3 thinks the entire sacrifice is too aberrant to produce a change of wind (if the sacrifice was meant to do so). For those who celebrate Polyxena's choice as glorious, see Grube 1941, 221; Conacher 1967, 150; Vellacott 1975, 192; Daitz 1971, 220; Matthaei 1918, 118.
27 Scholion on *Hecuba*, line 573.
28 Scodel 1996, 122 qualifies the view of Loraux 1987, 58–60 by pointing out that although warriors are struck in the breast, they do not offer their breast to piercing by a weapon.
29 For a possible ritual significance to Iphigenia's shedding of her robes, see Sourvinou-Inwood 1988, 127–35 and Thalmann 1993, 146.
30 Cohen 1997. Harlow 2000 suggested that Polyxena may here be appropriating heroic nudity along with a heroic defiance of death.
31 Rabinowitz 1993, 36–8, 57, 59; Kastely 1993, 1039; Gregory 1991, 98.
32 Mossman 1995, 144, 160; Scodel 1996, 125–6. Battezatto 2010, 74 thinks that by sacrificial logic Polyxena's free offer of her body assures her honorable treatment by the army.
33 Kastely 1993, 1039; Gregory 1991, 98, 113.

34 Mossman 1995, 60 and Gregory 1999, xvi note that Euripides seems to have deliberately marked the break between the play's two major actions with this exit.
35 See Collard 1991a, 166 for further bibliography on this scene.
36 Zeitlin 1991, 65; Gregory 1999, 134.
37 See Gregory 1991, 135 for this rebuttal.
38 See Collard 1991a, 170 on the rhetorical brilliance of the speech and Mossman 1995, 124, 125 on Hecuba's rhetorical flexibility and her new concern for society not just herself.
39 Nussbaum 1986 thinks the play shows how destroying convention (strictly human ethical standards) can destroy the stable character of those who rely on it. Daitz 1971, 223 notes the universalizing of ethics here.
40 Kovacs 1987, 101; Heath 1987a; Gregory 1991, 138-39; Segal 1993, 197; Mossman 1995, 182-3; Battezatto 2010, 88-99.
41 Heath 1987a, 67. Kerrigan 1996, 349-54 offers a particularly effective critique of Nussbaum 1986.
42 Translated W. Race 1997, Loeb Classical Library, Cambridge, Massachusetts: Harvard University Press.
43 Mercier 1993 offers a strong argument that Hecuba begins to supplicate Agamemnon at 752, reasserts her position at 787, resists his attempt to move his foot at 812-13, and very likely continues to cling to him until she is assured of his support around 888. By contrast, she may well give up supplicating Odysseus in the earlier scene, and Odysseus avoids supplication from Polyxena, although she refuses to do so. Zeitlin 1991, 77-8 equates Hecuba's supplication with Agamemnon's embrace of Cassandra.
44 This is the basis of Michelini's 1987 extensive criticism of Hecuba's rhetoric. Zeitlin 1991, 79 notes that Hecuba's turn to persuasion/sweet speaking adapts Odysseus' mode of speech. Kirkwood 1947, 67, n. 13 links Hecuba's *peithô* here with that she uses on Polymestor.
45 Conacher 1961, 22; Michelini 1987, 157; Segal 1993, 182; Nussbaum 1986, 414-15.

46 Harlow 2000 argues that Hecuba here symbolically usurps the male role of giving her daughter in marriage.
47 Segal 1993, 206.
48 Cited by Meridor 1983, 17–18. She argues (18–20) that Hecuba even hints at the crime of *hierosulia*, despoiling sacred shrines or rites, at 802–5.
49 Meridor 1983, 19; Collard 1991a, 185.
50 Burnett 1998, 169 enumerates violent revenges in various Greek myths.
51 Gregory 1991, 106 offers a defense of Hecuba's use of *charis* here as well within the norms of her culture. See Scodel 1998 on the blurred lines in such sexual relationships between slave and concubine and between rape and a consensual relationship.
52 On the move from *dikê* to *charis* also in speech to Odysseus, see Lloyd 1992, 96.
53 Kastely 1993, 1041. For those who think she succeeds in persuading Agamemnon here, see Kovacs 1987, 79, Heath 1987b, 147.

Chapter 5

1 Steiner 1994.
2 See Kovacs 1987, 104; Kastely 1993, 1043; and Collard 1991a, 27, who think that women are freer than men in this play. Daitz 1971, 222 on the other hand argues that although Polyxena was truly free, Polymestor is a slave to greed, Odysseus to the mob, Hecuba to her revenge, and the chorus to its survival.
3 Mossman 1995, 184 notes that these frightening mythical husband killers both went on to heterosexual activity or marriage and were not punished for their crimes.
4 Lloyd 1992, 95.
5 On exhilarating aspects of revenge, despite its putative destruction of nobility, see especially Reckford 1985, 118, who also notes the black comedy of the scene (Reckford 1991b, 30).

6 See note 4, chapter 3.
7 Thalmann 1993, 148; Segal 1993, 187.
8 Meridor 1978, 30 notes that Hecuba's use of *dikên didonai* and of *dikê* by Polymestor for what he suffers and Agamemnon's agreement suggests an official act of justice (see also Gregory 1991, 108–9).
9 On possible references to such Dionysiac myths in *Hecuba*, see Schlesier 1988, who argues for a reference to the destruction of the son (or wife and son) of the Thracian king Lycourgos after he resisted Dionysus, and Zeitlin 1991, 56. Mossman 1995, 167, n. 10 emphasizes the differences between the sane and deliberate women of this play and the maddened women of other Dionysiac myths.
10 Collard 1991b, 169; Zeitlin 1991 (1996 rev.), 181, 186; Gregory 1999, 176.
11 Zeitlin 1991, 71–4 with qualifications by Mossman 1995, 191.
12 Collard 1991a, 187; see also Hall 2006, 317–18. Burnett 1998, 170 notes that Polymestor is not allowed a lament over the children's bodies that might have stirred additional sympathy for him.
13 Collard 1991b, 168.
14 On the troubling role of Agamemnon as judge here, see Abrahamson 1952, 126–7; Hogan 1972, 254; Collard 1991a, 190; Luschnig 1976, 233; and Hall in Morwood and Hall, 2001, xxiii, who calls the 'trial' a 'kangaroo court' that has 'nothing to do with the administration of justice.' Polymestor's cries nevertheless require some action on Agamemnon's part. See Gregory 1999, 177; Kastely 1993, 1044; Lloyd 1992, 97.
15 On its rhetoric, see Lloyd 1992, 97; Buxton 1982, 181–2; Kovacs 1987, 107–8; Michelini, 1987, 156–7.
16 Mossman 1995, 175.
17 Michelini 1987, 157; Mossman 1995, 134 defends Hecuba's formal rhetoric in this speech.
18 Buxton 1982, 182.
19 Battezatto 2010, 82–83.

20 Hogan 1972, 256 emphasizes that the Greeks did think of Polymestor as friend and ally.
21 Adkins 1966, 203 stresses that Polymestor would have been justified if he acted as an ally, but in fact Hecuba shows that he acted for gold; Thalmann 1993, 149, n. 61 argues that this view ignores the death of Polymestor's children. Stanton 1995, 31 thinks that Hecuba's argument unfairly limits Polymestor's possible motives. In his view the play as a whole creates unresolved contradictions over respecting and adhering to traditional aristocratic values concerning *philia* and *xenia*. Rosenmeyer 1984–5 and Schubert 2000 among many others stress the way in which boundaries between friend and foe are repeatedly blurred in the play.
22 Lloyd 1992, 98.
23 Mossman 1995, 136.
24 Lloyd 1992, 98. Buxton 1982, 181 notes that to profess ignorance at speaking, as Hecuba did with Agamemnon earlier (814–19), is rhetorical; see also Lloyd 1992, 97.
25 Adkins 1966, 207–9.
26 Adkins 1966, 203–4.
27 Lloyd 1992, 96 views Hecuba as a defendant who is clearly in the right: 'Her rhetoric in the *agôn* is thus an instrument of justifiable self-defense, and not a significant means of revenge.'
28 Gregory 1999, xxix–xxxi. Contrary winds are mentioned at 898–901 and favorable winds at 1289–90. Achilles' ghost stopped the fleet (38), but it is not clear that he stopped the winds and the first choral ode addresses ocean breezes (444–6). However, gods are often said to control winds, and the shift in winds could convey a divine response. On the question of why the wind does not pick up after Polyxena's sacrifice, see the speculative views of Mitchell-Boyask 1993.
29 Kovacs 1987, 105 thinks that the change of wind shows divine favor to Hecuba; see also Heath 1987a, 67.
30 Meridor 1978, 30.

31 Zeitlin 1991, 64 thinks that the gaze of the star Seirios is transferred to the eyes of Hecuba as a dog. Burnett 1994, 152 argues that the dog's fiery glance is borrowed from the beacon that becomes her tomb.
32 Thalmann 1993, 150 thinks that Agamemnon fails to see that he has supported a crime that anticipates his own future at the hands of a woman.
33 For negative views, see Orban 1970; Rabinowitz 1993, 105, who emphasizes Hecuba's loss of speech; and Michelini 1987, 172–3, who stresses Hecuba's loss of her name.
34 For more positive assessments, see Burnett 1994 and 1998; Meridor 1978 and 1983; Gregory 1991, 110–12. Kovacs 1987, 108–9 argues that Hecuba's revenge is extreme but so is the crime that provoked it; heroism can be bestial and divine in the *Iliad*; there is no insanity and savagery in her words; her tomb becomes a source of awe. In Kovacs' view the Greeks are godless and without principle; Hecuba seeks justice and the gods enable her.
35 Burnett 1998, 172.
36 Burnett 1994, 152–3; Gregory 1999, xxxiv. Mossman 1995, 196–8 sees the figure of the dog as ambivalent but the metamorphosis releases Hecuba from suffering (199). Kovacs 1987, 108–9, adds that Hecuba is no longer a slave.
37 Burnett 1994, 159. Gellie 1980, 36 thinks the revenge is too pleasurable and Polymester too evil for the play to offer an example of moral disintegration. The play is not a tragedy and the final aetiology offers in his view a postscript, not a judgment on the revenge (40). In my view, it is not obvious that Agamemnon's fate is a logical result of the action of the play.
38 Burnett 1994, 155, 156.
39 Zeitlin 1991, 94, n. 40.
40 Burnett 1994, 162 points out that Hecuba needs to become a dog to inhabit this landmark and Euripides probably invented this metamorphosis for this purpose. Burnett 1998, 174–5 notes that at Euripides' *Electra* 586 Orestes is compared to a beacon sign.

The phrase 'wild justice' is borrowed from Francis Bacon's essay *Of Revenge*. For Meridor 1978, 33–4 the metamorphosis is not necessarily a moral evaluation. The transformation of Cadmus and Harmonia into serpents at *Bacchae* 1330–8 offers a similar case.

Chapter 6

1. On choral identity in Greek tragedy, see Gould 1996 and Foley 2003 with further bibliography.
2. See Collard 1989–90; Rosivach 1975; Michelini 1987 on the chorus' attempt at collective detachment from its own woes, on its self-absorption, its focus on unreal hopes and survival. Michelini 1987, 330 notes the 'remote and fantasied quality' of their songs.
3. Rosivach 1975, 359.
4. Rosivach 1975, 354, 358 and Michelini 1987, 331–2 discuss the incompatibility between the women's role as foreign slaves and their aspirations to participate in cults exclusive to virgins. Mossman 1995, 81 notes the ornate language and convoluted word order used to describe weaving the *peplos* (robe) for Athena.
5. Zeitlin 1991, 76 comments on the move from present to past.
6. See Collard 1991a, 164 on this ode and the elaborate interlacing of the word order in 631–34 that evokes the encirclement of fate; Collard 1989–90, 90 notes the rarity of enjambed epodes in tragedy. Dale 1983, 214 compares the pairing of a mimetic strophe to a moralizing antistrophe to Euripides' *Bacchae* 977–1010.
7. Mossman 1995, 85.
8. Collard 1989–90, 89. This meter is common in later so-called 'dithyrambic' odes of Euripides (Kranz 1933), which tend to be mannered, decorative, and tangential to the main action (Collard 1991a, 178).

9 Some editors delete these lines.
10 Mitchell-Boyask 1993, 126.

Chapter 7

1 Translated J. H. Freese 1926, Loeb Classical Library, Cambridge, MA: Harvard University Press.
2 Translated Finley 1951.
3 Blundell 1989, 55.
4 Mossman 1995, 77. See her additional examples on 172–5.
5 Heath 1987a.
6 Heath 1987a, 40–3.
7 See Mossman 1995, 220–1, who also notes the elegant translation of the prologue by Francesco Filefo in 1461.
8 Mossman 1995, 220–5. Pollard 2012,1064 cites thirty-seven individual or partial editions in the sixteenth century and seven vernacular editions.
9 Sixteenth-century writers such as Ariosto and Rabelais show definite knowledge of the text of *Hecuba* (Mossman 1995, 228).
10 Translated by F. J. Miller 1916, Loeb Classical Library, Cambridge, MA: Harvard University Press.
11 Fontinoy 1955.
12 Pollard 2010.
13 See Mossman 1995, 236–41 on some of these points.
14 Here he was supported by J. C. Scaliger, whose *Poetics* was published after his death at Lyons in 1561 and at Leyden in 1581, and Minturno 1564 (Pollard 2012, 1065).
15 Heath 1987a, 46.
16 Scaliger 1905, 61.
17 Heath 1987a, 47 and Mossman 1995, 234, 242. No one during the Renaissance objected to Hecuba's role as an avenging woman, especially because she is old and thus asexual. In new Renaissance revenge plays, the avenger was generally male.

Pollard 2012, 1068 nevertheless suggests that Hecuba's appeal for the Renaissance lay in her femininity.
18 Pollard 2012, 1066.
19 See Schlegel 1876, 137. See also the edition of *Hecuba* by G. Hermannus, 1831, xvii.
20 The final scene of *Medea* includes questioning of the heroine's revenge by Jason.
21 Kerrigan 1996, 21; Michelini 1987, 170.
22 Kerrigan 1996, 29.
23 Zeitlin 1991, 82–3. See also Battezatto 2010, especially 100.
24 Foley 2001.
25 See further, Heath 1987a, 42.
26 Foley 2001, 276. See also Nussbaum 1986, 417 on women's vulnerability to chance.
27 Foley 2001, 296.

Chapter 8

1 See the Archive for Performances of Greek and Roman Drama (www.apgrd.ox.ac.uk) at Oxford for further details on all these early performances. On the early French reception of the play, see Garnier 1999.
2 See Hall and Macintosh 2005, 64, 66, 80, 84–5, 97 on West and Delap.
3 See Hall and Macintosh 2005, 255, 258, 366, 386 on Valpy and Metcalfe. See also Metcalfe 1893.
4 Lister 1938.
5 Crane 1952.
6 The chorus does, however, briefly lament Achilles as well.
7 This description is based on a performance taped for the Dance in America series on US public television; it was made available on Pyramid Film and Video in 1969. See also Stodelle 1984.
8 In *Trojan Women* Helen actually debates the queen.

9   For more detail, see the reviews by Jackie Horwitz, *Santa Monica Evening Outlook*, 16 January 1987; Jeff Rubio, *The Orange County Register*, 27 January 1987; Sylvie Drake, *Los Angeles Times*, 3 January 1987; Janice Arkatov, *Los Angeles Times*, 6 January 1987; Richard Stayton, *Los Angeles Herald Examiner*, 14 January 1987; see also Hartigan 1995, 140–1.
10 Review by Marianne McDonald, http://www.didaskalia.net/issues/vol2no3/contents.html.
11 Robert Hurwitt, *San Francisco Examiner*, 22 October 1998 thought the second production succeeded in unifying the play around Hecuba's shift from agony to righteous revenge.
12 Chad Jones, *The Oakland Tribune*, 20 and 23 October 1998 and *San Mateo Co. Times*, 3 October 1998: 'it's a relief, then, when Hecuba switches into revenge mode.'
13 Roberta Floden, *Marin Independent Journal*, 23 October 1998.
14 Leo Stutzln, *The Modesto Bee*, 25 October 1998.
15 Bob Graham, *San Francisco Chronicle*, 21 October 1998.
16 Dennis Harvey, http://sanfrancisco.sidewalk.com/detail/55470.
17 For the published translation, see Nelson 1997. For largely favorable reviews, see Pamela Sommers, *The Washington Post*, 11 November 1998; Sarah Kaufman, *The Washington Post*, 20 November 1998; and Bob Mondello, *City Paper*, 13 November 1998. Sommers called Collins 'a Jessye Norman stripped of her vocal gifts.' The translation also received a strong response. A video of the performance is available at the Washington Area Performing Arts Video Archive.
18 McGuiness 2004.
19 Many of the 2004 performances mentioned the Beslan school tragedy in Russia's Caucusus as influential for the productions.
20 For reviews of these recent British productions, see The Reception of Classical Texts project, www2.open.ac.uk/ClassicalStudies/GreekPlays. See also Hardwick 2007.
21 Susannah Clapp, *Observer*, 19 September 2004. See Hardwick 2007, 100 on the parody of *xenia* or guest friendship in this production.

22 Harrison 2005.
23 Mark Shenton, *Sunday Express*, 10 April 2005.
24 See for example Susannah Clapp, BBC Radio, 8 April 2005. Neil Genzlinger, *New York Times*, 25 January 2006; Charles Isherwood, *New York Times*, 20 June 2005; and Michael Feingold, *Village Voice*, 21 June 2005 offer helpful reviews of the BAM production.
25 Mark Lawson, *The Tablet*, 16 April 2005 and Hardwick 2007, 98.
26 McLeish 1995.
27 David Murray, *The Financial Times*, 8 September 1992.
28 Paul Taylor, *The Independent*, 11 September 1992.
29 Paul Taylor, *The Independent*, 11 September 1992.
30 Arrowsmith 1958 served the rhetoric of this production effectively.
31 Gwen Orel, www.theatrescene.net/ts%5Carticles.nsf/0/ E82DE4E)CDD2B4B985256F3900271D44?OpenDocument, Gyda Arber, nytheatre.com/nytheatre/hecuba564.htm and Charles McNulty, *Village Voice*, 19 October 2004, stressed the play's debasement of language and the warping of democratic values; Dan Bacalzo gave the play a largely critical review, www.theatermania.com/content/news.cfm/story/5217. (All accessed 17 May 2005).
32 Lorna Hardwick, 11 November 2004, www2.open.ac.uk/ ClassicalStudies/GreekPlays.
33 Jennie Webb, www.backstage.com, 27 May 2004. See further www4.open.ac.uk/csdb/ASP/ViewBook.asp, 14 and 16.
34 McDonald 2005. Jennifer de Poyen, *San Diego Union-Tribune*, 22 November 2004.
35 Carson 2006. See Dinitia Smith, *New York Times* 14 November 2004.
36 Robert Nesti, *Boston Herald*, 22 September 2004 and Ryan McKittrick, *Boston Globe*, 24 September 2004.
37 See especially the 1995 production of *Hekabe* by the RO Theater in Rotterdam, Arnheim and Eindhoven, North Brabant, Netherlands, translated by Gerard Koolschijn, directed by Peter

de Baan, http://www.didaskalia.net/issues/vol2no2/hekabe.html, and the 1999 performance of *Hekabe* translated by Michael Wachsmann and directed by Dieter Dorn at the Münchner Kammerspiele Schauspielhaus starring Gisela Stein with reviews in the research collection at www.apgrd.ox.ac.uk.

Bibliography

Abrahamson, E. 'Euripides' Tragedy of *Hecuba*,' *Transactions and Proceedings of the American Philological Association* 83: 120–9 (1952).

Adkins, A. A. 'Basic Greek Values in Euripides' *Hecuba* and *Hercules Furens*,' *Classical Quarterly* 16, no. 2: 193–216 (1966).

Battezatto, L. *Euripide Ecuba*. Milano: BUR (Rizzoli), 2010.

Biehl, W. *Textkritik and Formanalyse zur euripideischen Hekabe. Ein Beitrag zum Verständnis der Komposition*. Heidelberg: Universitäts Verlag C. Winter, 1997.

Billing, C. M. 'Lament and Revenge in the *Hekabe* of Euripides,' *New Theatre Quarterly* 23, no. 1: 49–57 (2007).

Blundell, M. W. *Helping Friends and Harming Enemies: A Study in Sophocles and Greek Ethics*. Cambridge: Cambridge University Press, 1989.

Brilliante, C. 'Sul Prologo dell'*Ecuba* di Euripide,' *Rivista di Filologia e di Instruzione Classica* 116: 429–47 (1988).

Burkert, W. *Greek Religion*, translated J. Raffan. Cambridge, MA: Harvard University Press, 1985.

Burnett, A. P. 'Hekabe the Dog,' *Arethusa* 27: 151–64 (1994).

Burnett, A. P. *Revenge in Attic and Later Tragedy*. Berkeley and Los Angeles, CA: University of California Press, 1998.

Buxton, R. G. A. *Persuasion in Greek Tragedy: A Study of Peitho*. Cambridge: Cambridge University Press, 1982.

Cohen, D. *Law, Violence, and Community in Classical Athens*. Cambridge: Cambridge University Press, 1995.

Cohen, V. 'Divesting the Female Breast of Clothes in Classical Sculpture'. In A. O. Koloski-Ostrow and C. L. Lyons (eds), *Naked Truths: Women, Sexuality and Gender in Classical Art and Archaeology*, 66–92. London and New York: Routledge, 1997.

Collard, C. 'Formal Debates in Euripides' Drama,' *Greece and Rome* 22, no. 1: 58–71 (1975). Reproduced with addendum in

J. Mossman (ed.), *Euripides*, 64–80. Oxford: Oxford University Press, 2003.

Collard, C. 'The Stasimon Euripides, *Hecuba* 905–52,' *Sacris Eruditi* 31: 85–97 (1989–90).

Collard, C. (trans. and comm.) *Euripides Hecuba*. Warminster: Aris and Phillips, 1991a.

Collard, C. 'Monody of the Blinded Polymestor.' In J. A. López Férez (ed.), *Estudios Actuales sobre Textos Griegos*, 161–73. Madrid: Ediciones Cátedra, 1991b.

Collinge, N. E. '*Hecuba* 925–26,' *Classical Philology* 49: 35–36 (1954).

Conacher, D. J. 'Euripides' *Hecuba*,' *American Journal of Philology* 82: 1–26 (1961).

Conacher, D. J. *Euripidean Drama: Myth, Theme, and Structure*. Toronto: University of Toronto Press, 1967.

Crane, B. *The House of Atreus: Three Dramas in One Act*. Boston, MA: Walter H. Baker Company, 1952.

Cribiore, R. 'The Grammarian's Choice: the Popularity of Euripides' *Phoenissae* in Hellenistic and Roman Education.' In Y. L. Too (ed.), *Education in Greek and Roman Antiquity*, 241–59. Leiden, Boston, Köln: Brill, 2001.

Cropp, M. and G. Fick. *Resolutions and Chronology in Euripides*. *Bulletin of the Institute of Classical Studies*, Supplement 43. London: Institute of Classical Studies, 1985.

Csapo, E. 'The Men Who Built Theatres.' In P. Wilson (ed.), *The Greek Theatre and Festivals: Documentary Studies*, including Appendix by Hans R. Goette, 87–121. Oxford: Oxford University Press, 2000.

Csapo, E. and W. J. Slater. *The Context of Ancient Drama*. Ann Arbor, MI: University of Michigan Press, 1995.

Daitz, S. 'Concepts of Freedom and Slavery in Euripides' *Hecuba*,' *Hermes* 99: 217–26 (1971).

Dale, A. M. 'Metrical Analyses of Tragic Choruses,' *Bulletin of the Institute of Classical Studies Supplement* 21, no. 3: 63–5 (1983) and 21, no. 1: 76–7 (1971).

Delebecque, É. *Euripide et la guerre du Péloponnèse* (Études et Commentaires x). Paris: Klincksieck, 1951.

Della Corte, F., 'Il Polidoro Euripides.' *Dioniso* 36: 5–14 (1962).

Diggle, J. 'Notes on the *Hecuba* of Euripides,' *Greek, Roman, and Byzantine Studies* 23: 315–23 (1982).

Dunn, F. M. *Tragedy's End: Closure and Innovation in Euripidean Drama*. New York: Oxford University Press, 1996.

Durand, J.-L. and F. Lissarrague. 'Mourir à l'autel', *Archiv für Religionsgeschichte* 1: 83–106 (1999).

Erbse, H. *Studien zum Prolog der Euripideischen Tragödie*. I, no. 3: 48–59. Berlin: W. De Gruyter, 1984.

Ferrari, F. 'In margine all' *Ecuba*,' *Annali della Scuola Normale Superiore Pisa* 15: 45–49 (1985).

Finley Jr., J. H. *Thucydides: The Peloponnesian War*. New York: Modern Library, 1951.

Fitzgerald, G. 'Euripides and Hecuba. Confounding the "Model",' *Maia* 41: 217–22 (1989).

Foley, H. P. *Female Acts in Greek Tragedy*. Princeton, NJ: Princeton University Press, 2001.

Foley, H. P. 'Choral Identity in Greek Tragedy,' *Classical Philology* 98, no. 1: 1–30 (2003).

Fontinoy, C. 'Le sacrifice nuptial de Polyxène,' *Antiquité Classique* 19, no. 2: 383–96 (1955).

Gantz, T. *Early Greek Myth*. Baltimore, MD: Johns Hopkins University Press, 1993.

Garnier, B. *Pour une poétique de la traduction: L'Hécube d'Euripide en France de la traduction humaniste à la tragédie classique*. Paris: L'Harmatttan, 1999.

Gellie, G. 'Hecuba and Tragedy,' *Antichthon* 14: 30–44 (1980).

Goldhill, S. D. 'The Great Dionysia and Civic Ideology,' *Journal of Hellenic Studies* 107: 58–76 (1987).

Goldhill, S. D. 'Representing Democracy: Women at the Great Dionysia.' In R. Osborne and S. Hornblower (eds), *Ritual, Finance, Politics: Athenian Democratic Accounts Presented to David Lewis*, 347–69. Oxford: Oxford University Press, 1994.

Gould, J. 'Tragedy and Collective Experience.' In M. S. Silk (ed.), *Tragedy and the Tragic. Greek Theatre and Beyond*, 217–43. Oxford: Oxford University Press, 1996.

Gregory, J. *Euripides and the Instruction of the Athenians*. Ann Arbor, MI: University of Michigan Press, 1991.

Gregory, J. 'Euripides, *Hecuba* 54', *Phoenix* 46: 266–9 (1992).

Gregory, J. 'Genealogy and Intertextuality in *Hecuba*,' *The American Journal of Philology* 116, no. 3: 389–97 (1995).

Gregory, J. (ed. and comm.) *Euripides Hecuba. Introduction, Text, and Commentary*. Atlanta, GA: Scholar's Press, 1999.

Grube, G. M. A. *The Drama of Euripides*. London: Methuen, 1941.

Hall, E. *Inventing the Barbarian: Greek Self-definition through Tragedy*. Oxford: Oxford University Press, 1989.

Hall, E. 'Singing Roles in Tragedy.' In E. Hall, *The Theatrical Cast of Athens*, 288–320. Oxford: Oxford University Press, 2006.

Hall, E. and F. Macintosh. *Greek Tragedy and the British Theatre 1660–1914*. Oxford: Oxford University Press, 2005.

Halleran, M. R. *Stagecraft in Euripides*. London: Croom Helm, 1985.

Harder, R. E. *Die Frauenrollen bei Euripides*. Stuttgart: B. Metziersche Verlagsbuchhandlung und Carl Ernst Poeschel Verlag GmbH, 1993.

Hardwick, L. 'Decolonizing the Mind? Controversial Productions of Greek Drama in Post-colonial England, Scotland, and Ireland.' In C. Stray (ed.), *Remaking the Classics: Literature, Genre and Media in Britain 1800–2000*, 89–105. London: Duckworth, 2007.

Harlow, D. 'Euripides and the Male Heroic Code, Senior Essay, Barnard College, New York, (2000).

Hartigan, K. *Greek Tragedy on the American Stage: Ancient Drama in the Commercial Theatre, 1882–1994*. Westport, CT and London: Greenwood Press, 1995.

Heath, M. '*Jure principen locum tenet*. Euripides' *Hecuba*,' *Bulletin of the Institute of Classical Studies* 34: 40–68 (1987a).

Heath, M. *The Poetics of Greek Tragedy*. Stanford, CA: Stanford University Press, 1987b.

Henderson, J. 'Women and the Athenian Dramatic Festivals,' *Transactions and Proceedings of the American Philological Society* 121: 133–47 (1991).

Herman, G. *Ritualized Friendship in the Greek City*. Cambridge: Cambridge University Press, 1987.

Herman, G. 'How Violent was Athenian Society?' In R. Osborne and S. Hornblower (eds), *Ritual, Finance, Politics: Athenian Democratic Accounts Presented to David Lewis*, 99–117. Oxford: Oxford University Press, 1994.

Herman, G. 'Honour, Revenge, and the State in Fourth-century Athens.' In W. Eder (ed.), *Die Athenische Demokratie im 4. Jahrhundert v. Chri. Vollendung oder verfall einer Verfassungsform?*, 43–66. Stuttgart: Franz Steiner Verlag, 1995.

Hermannus, G. (ed.) *Euripidis Hecuba*. Leipzig: Weidemann, 1831.

Hogan, J. C. 'Thucydides 3.52–68 and Euripides' *Hecuba*,' *Phoenix* 26: 241–57 (1972).

Holzman, S. 'Interpreting the Great Kizoldun Sarcophagus.' Cambridge: Cambridge MPhil thesis, 2012.

Hose, M. *Studien zum Chor bei Euripides*, 2 vols. Stuttgart: B. G. Teubner, 1990–1.

Jouanna, J. 'Réalité et théâtralité du rêve: le rêve dans l'*Hecuba* d'Euripide,' *Ktema* 7: 43–52 (1982).

Kastely, J. L. 'Rhetoric and Violence in Euripides' *Hecuba*,' *Proceedings of the Modern Language Association* 108, no. 5: 1036–49 (1993).

Kerrigan, J. *Revenge Tragedy: Aeschylus to Armageddon*. Oxford: Oxford University Press, 1996.

King, K. C. 'The Politics of Imitation: Euripides' *Hekabe* and the Homeric Achilles,' *Arethusa* 18: 47–66 (1985).

Kirkwood, G. M. 'Hecuba and Nomos,' *Transactions and Proceedings of the American Philological Association* 78: 61–68 (1947).

Kitto, H. D. F. *Greek Tragedy: A Literary Study*. London: Methuen, 1961, 1971.

Kovacs, D. *The Heroic Muse. Studies in the Hippolytus and Hecuba of Euripides*. Baltimore, MD: Johns Hopkins University Press, 1987.

Kranz, W. *Stasimon*. Berlin: Weidmann, 1933.

Lane, N. 'Staging Polydoros' Ghost in the Prologue of Euripides' *Hecuba*,' *Classical Quarterly* 57, no. 1: 290–4 (2007).

Ley, G. 'The Date of the *Hecuba*,' *Eranos* 85: 216–29 (1987).

Lister, H. B. *The Bride of a Ghost* or *Polyxena*. La Bohème Club of San Francisco, 1938.

Lloyd, M. *The Agon in Euripides*. Oxford: Oxford University Press, 1992.

Loraux, N. *The Invention of Athens: The Funeral Oration in the Classical City* (trans. Alan Sheridan). Cambridge, MA: Harvard University Press, 1986 (originally Paris 1981).

Loraux, N. *Tragic Ways of Killing a Woman* (trans. Anthony Forster). Cambridge, MA: Harvard University Press, 1987 (originally Paris 1985).

Luschnig, C. A. E. 'Euripides' *Hekabe*: The Time is Out of Joint,' *Classical Journal* 71, no. 3: 227–41 (1976).

MacDowell, D. M. *The Law in Classical Athens*. Ithaca, NY: Cornell University Press, 1978.

Marshall, C. W. 'The Costume of Hecuba's Attendants,' *Acta Classica* 44: 127–36 (2001).

Matthaei, L. E. *Studies in Greek Tragedy*. Cambridge: Cambridge University Press, 1918.

Matthiessen, K. *Studien zur Textüberlieferung der Hekabe des Euripides*. Heidelberg: C. Winter, 1974.

Mercier, C. E. 'Suppliant Ritual in Euripidean Tragedy,' Dissertation, Columbia University (1990)

Mercier, C. E. 'Hekabe's Extended Supplication (*Hek.* 752–888),' *Transactions and Proceedings of the American Philological Association* 123: 149–60 (1993).

Meridor, R. 'Hecuba's Revenge: Some Observations on Euripides' *Hecuba*,' *American Journal of Philology* 99, no. 1: 28–35 (1978).

Meridor, R. 'The Function of Polymestor's Crime in the *Hecuba* of Euripides,' *Eranos* 8: 13–20 (1983).

Metcalfe, C. *Hecuba a la Mode: The Wily Greek and the Modest Maid*. London, 1893.

Michelini, A. *Euripides and the Tragic Paradox*. Madison, WI: University of Wisconsin Press, 1987.

Minturno, A. *L'Arte Poetica*. Venice, 1564.

Mitchell-Boyask, R. 'Sacrifice and Revenge in Euripides' *Hecuba*,' *Ramus* 22, no. 2: 116–34 (1993).

Montanari, F. 'Un "Nuovo Papiro dell'Ecuba di Euripides (P. Tebt. 683 Recto",' *Rivista di Filologia e di Instruzione Classica* 115: 24–32 (1987).

Mossman, J. *Wild Justice: A Study of Euripides' Hecuba*. Oxford: Oxford University Press, 1995.

Neer, R. 'A tomb both great and blameless: Marriage and murder on a sarcophagus from the Hellespont,' *Res: Anthropology and Aesthetics* 61/62: 98–115 (2012).

Nussbaum, M. *The Fragility of Goodness*. Cambridge: Cambridge University Press, 1986.

O'Connor-Visser, E. A. M. E. *Aspects of Human Sacrifice in the Tragedies of Euripides*. Amsterdam: B. R. Grüner, 1987.

Orban, M. 'Hécube, Drame Humain,' *Les Etudes Classiques* 38: 316–30 (1970).

Pagani, G. 'Il dramma di Polissena nell' *Ecuba* di Euripide,' *Dioniso* 44: 46–63 (1970).

Palima, M. (trans.) *Dante Alighieri. The Inferno*. New York and London: W. W. Norton, 2002.

Perdicoyianni, H. 'Le vocabulaire de la douleur dans l'*Hécube* et *Les Troyennes* d'Euripide,' *Les Études Classiques* 61: 195–204 (1993).

Pohlenz, M. *Die griechische Tragödie*, 2 vols. Göttingen: Vandenhoeck and Ruprecht, 1954.

Pollard, T. 'Tragedy and Revenge.' In E. Smith and G. A. Sullivan, Jr (eds), *The Cambridge Companion to English Renaissance Tragedy*, 58–72. Cambridge: Cambridge University Press, 2010.

Pollard, T. 'What's Hecuba to Shakespeare?,' *Renaissance Quarterly* 65, no. 4: 1060–93 (2012).

Quasimodo, S. '*Ecuba*,' *Dioniso* 36: 89–97 (1962).

Rabinowitz, N. S. *Anxiety Veiled: Euripides and the Traffic in Women*. Ithaka, NY and London: Cornell University Press, 1993.

Reckford, K. J. 'Concepts of Demoralization in the *Hecuba*.' In P. Burian (ed.), *Directions in Euripidean Criticism*, 112–28. Durham, NC: Duke University Press, 1985.

Reckford, K. J. 'Introduction to *Euripides' Hecuba*.' In J. Lembke and K. J. Reckford, *Euripides Hecuba*, 3–20. Oxford: Oxford University Press, 1991a.

Reckford, K. J. 'Pity and Terror in Euripides' *Hecuba*,' *Arion* 1, no. 2: 24–43 (1991b).

Riedweg, C. 'Der Tragödiendichter als Rhetor? Redestrategien in Euripides' *Hekabe* und ihr Verhältnis zur zeitgenössischen Rhetoriktheorie,' *Rheinishes Museum* 143, no. 1: 1–31 (2000).

Rose, C. B. *Archaeology of Greek and Roman Troy*. New York: Cambridge University Press, 2013.

Roselli, D. *Theater of the People*. Austin, TX: University of Texas Press, 2011.

Rosenmeyer, T. G. 'Euripides' "*Hecuba*": Horror Story or Tragedy,' First International Meeting of Ancient Greek Drama: Delphi 8–12 April 1984, Delphi 4–25 June 1985 (Athens 1987): 264–70 (1984–5).

Rosivach, V. J. 'The First Stasimon of the *Hecuba*,' *American Journal of Philology* 96, no. 4: 349–62 (1975).

Scaliger, J. C. *Select Translations from Scaliger's Poetics* (ed. and trans. F. M. Padelford). New York: H. Holt, 1905.

Schlegel, A. W. *Lectures on Dramatic Art and Literature* (trans. J. Black, rev. A.J.W. Morrison). London: G. Bell and Sons, 1876 (originally published Heidelberg, 1809–11).

Schlesier, R. 'Die Bakchen des Hades: Dionysische Aspekte von Euripides' *Hekabe*,' *Métis* 3, no. 1–2: 111–35 (1988).

Schubert, P. 'L'*Hécube* d'Euripide et la définition de l'étranger,' *Quaderni Urbinati di Cultura Classica* 64, no. 1: 87–100 (2000).

Scodel, R. '*Domôn Agalma*: Virgin Sacrifice and Aesthetic Object,' *Transactions and Proceedings of the American Philological Association* 126: 111–28 (1996).

Scodel, R. 'The Captive's Dilemma: Sexual Acquiescence in Euripides'

Hecuba and Troades,' *Harvard Studies in Classical Philology* 98: 137–54 (1998).

Seaford, R. A. S. 'The Date of Euripides' *Cyclops*,' *Journal of Hellenic Studies* 102: 161–72 (1982).

Segal, C. *Euripides and the Poetics of Sorrow*. Durham, NC: Duke University Press, 1993.

Sevinç, N. 'A New Sarcophagus of Polyxena from the Salvage Excavations at Gümşüçay,' *Studia Troica* 6: 251–64 (1996).

Sourvinou-Inwood, C. *Studies in Girl's Transitions: Aspects of the Arkteia and Age Representations in Attic Iconography*. Athens: Kardamitsa, 1988.

Stanton, G. R. 'Aristocratic Obligation in Euripides' *Hekabe*,' *Mnemosyne* 48, no. 1: 11–33 (1995).

Steidle, W. 'Zur *Hekabe* des Euripides,' *Weiner Studien* 79: 133–42 (1966).

Steiner, D. T. *The Tyrant's Writ: Myths and Images of Writing in Ancient Greece*. Princeton, NJ: Princeton University Press, 1994.

Stiblinus, G. *Euripides Poeta Tragicorum Princeps*. Basel, 1562.

Stodelle, E. *Deep Song: The Dance Story of Martha Graham*. New York and London: Schirmer and Collier Macmillan, 1984.

Strohm, H. *Euripides: Interpretationen zur Dramtischen Form*. Munich: Beck, 1957.

Synodinou, K. 'Manipulation of Patriotic Convention by Odysseus in the *Hecuba*,' *Métis* 9, no. 9–10: 189–96 (1994–95).

Tarkow, T. A. 'Tragedy and Transformation: Parent and Child in Euripides' *Hecuba*,' *Maia* 36: 123–36 (1984).

Tetsall, R. 'An Instance of "Surprise" in the *Hecuba*,' *Mnemosyne* 7: 340–1 (1954).

Thalmann, W. 'Euripides and Aeschylus: the Case of *The Hekabe*,' *Classical Antiquity* 12, no. 1: 126–59 (1993).

Vellacott, P. *Ironic Drama*. Cambridge: Cambridge University Press, 1975.

Wiles, D. *Tragedy in Athens*. Cambridge: Cambridge University Press, 1997.

Wilkins, J. 'The State and the Individual: Euripides' Plays of Voluntary Self-sacrifice.' In A. Powell (ed.), *Euripides, Women and Sexuality*, 177–94. London and New York: Routledge, 1990.

Yunis, H. *A New Creed: Fundamental Religious Beliefs in the Athenian Polis and Euripidean Drama*. Göttingen: Vandenhoeck & Ruprecht, 1988.

Zeitlin, F. I. 'Euripides' *Hekabe* and the Somatics of Dionysiac Drama,' *Ramus* 20, no. 1: 53–94 (1991); revised in 1996 in her *Playing the Other: Gender and Society in Classical Greek Literature*, 172–218. Chicago, IL: University of Chicago Press.

Index

Achilles, 39–41; ghost of, 1–2, 37, 79; and Hecuba, 21, 68; and Iphigenia, 114n22; and Patroclus, 16, 113n19; and Polyxena, 20, 44, 79, 117n6; tomb of, 18–20
Adkins, A. A., 118n17, 123n21
Aegeus, 52
Aeneid (Vergil), 70, 114n21
aeolo-choriambic meter, 63
Aeschylus, 14, 68; *Agamemnon*, 16, 44, 52–3, 79, 112n14; *Eumenides*, 35, 59; *Liberation Bearers*, 35; *Persians*, 35, 53
African Continuum Theater Company (ACTCo), 85–6
Agamemnon, 21, 67; and Cassandra, 1, 15, 27, 48; fate of, 29, 58–9, 124n32, 124n37; and Hecuba, 15–16, 27–8, 46–50, 55–60, 120n43; and Iphigenia, 16, 20; and Polymestor, 116n18
agôn (debate), 6, 123n27; between Agamemnon and Hecuba, 55–60; between Odysseus and Hecuba, 38–41. *See also* rhetoric
Ajax (Sophocles), 5, 40, 49, 50, 74
alastôr (avenging spirit), 45, 65
Alcestis (Euripides), 71
Alexander of Pherae, 3
Algeria, 9
Ambrosino, John, 90
anapestic meter, 61
Andromache, 15, 37, 81, 113n18
Andromache (Euripides), 3, 67
Antigone (Sophocles), 5, 58, 71, 74
Archive of Performances of Greek and Roman Drama (APGRD), 127n1
aretê (virtue), 118n17

Argentinian *desaparecidos*, 9
Ariosto, Ludovico, 126n9
Aristophanes, 3; *Clouds*, 3; *Frogs*, 111n2; *Gerytades*, 36
Aristotle, 74; *Poetics*, 29, 33, 70–2; *Rhetoric*, 3, 68
Arrowsmith, William, 89
Artemis, 62, 63, 65
Astyanax, 1, 15, 70, 81, 114n20
Athena, 15, 16, 44, 59, 63, 64; *peplos* of, 62, 125n4
atrocitas (tragic horror), 70

Babcock, Jadwiga, 80
Bacchae (Euripides), 14, 53, 125n40; poetic devices in, 125n4; as revenge tragedy, 67
bacchic song, 27, 45, 53
Bacon, Francis, 125n40
barbarians, 27, 32, 57, 63; Odysseus on, 40, 41, 56; revenge by, 49–50, 54; Thracians as, 21–2, 59
Battezzato, L., 119n32
Battle of Algiers (film), 9
Before the Rain (film), 72
body, as theme in *Hecuba*, 34, 45, 48, 57–8, 123n28–29
Boeotia, 5
Bosseau, Remi Barclay, 83
Boswell, Laurence, 87–9
Bride of a Ghost (Lister), 78–9
Brygos Painter, the, 114n20
burial rites, 5, 9, 30, 56–8, 59, 74
Burnett, Anne, 59, 60, 113n8, 124n31; on Hecuba transformed into dog, 124n40
Bush, George W., 88
Buxton, Richard, 32
Byzantine triad, of Euripides' plays, xiii, 3, 67

Çanakkale sarcophagus, 18, 19, 44
Carson, Anne, 90
Cassandra, 37, 44; and Agamemnon, 1, 15, 27, 48; fate of, 29, 58; in *Trojan Women,* 15, 21, 49–50
Castle, Diana, 90
Catullus, 114n21
Cave of the Heart (Graham), 81
charis (reciprocity), 38–41, 48–50, 55, 121nn51–52
Children of Heracles (Euripides), 42, 52, 67
chitôn (robe), 18, 19, 44
chorus, 11–14, 40–1, 53–4, 57; in artwork, 18–20, 35; Burnett on, 113n8; odes sung by, 26–8, 34, 43, 61–5; in modern productions, 81–2, 86, 88, 90
Clytemnestra (Graham), 81
Collard, Christopher, 54, 116n14
Collins, Cheryl, 86
Cooke, Naomi, 90
Corcyra, 7
Cortege of Eagles (Graham), 80–1
Crane, Burton, 79, 80
Critias, 47
Cyclops (Euripides), 14, 53
Cynossema, 21, 29, 33, 58–60, 114n28, 124n31, 124n34

dactylo-epitrite meter, 64
Daedalus, 48
Daitz, S., 121n2
Danaids, 9, 51
Dante Alighieri, 3–4
Darius Painter, the, 53
dating, of *Cyclops,* 14; of *Hecuba,* 4, 14, 92; of *Trojan Women,* 15, 92
debates. *See agôn*
Delap, John, 77
Demophon, 52
Demosthenes, 3, 13
Dictys of Crete, 114n21, 114n28
dikê (punishment), 32, 53, 58, 74, 122n8; and *charis,* 40, 41, 48, 121n52; *tôi dikaiôi,* 39. *See also* justice
Dionysus, 23, 53, 58, 122n9; cults of, 22; festivals of, 11–12
dithyrambs, 11–12, 125n8
dochmiac meter, 45, 53, 65
dreams, 25, 36, 37
D'Silva, Darrell, 88
Dukakis, Olympia, 82–5

Eastwood, Clint, 72
Egyptian Danaids, 9, 51
Electra (Euripides), 67, 71, 124n40
Electra (Sophocles), 71, 79
Emery, Esther, 90
Ennius, 3, 114n21
Erasmus, Desiderius, 69, 77
Erectheus (Euripides), 42

Fitzgerald, G., 115n5
freedom, 121n2
Friendly Fire Productions, 89
friendship. *See philia*

Gellie, G., 124n37
gender roles, 13, 63; manipulation of, 33, 49, 52, 84; and marriage, 121n46; and religious rites, 8, 125n4; and revenge, 32, 51, 126n17. *See also* women
geras (prize), 20; Polyxena as, 35, 37, 117n6
ghost(s), 35–6, 78–9; of Achilles, 1–2, 37, 79; of King Darius, 35; of Polydorus, 5, 13, 25, 35–6
Gigantomachy, 62
gods, 9, 36, 38, 46–8, 63
Graham, Martha, 80–1
Greek theater, 11–14
Gregory, J., 112n10, 116n15
guest friendship. *See xenia*

Hades, 36, 44, 53
Hamlet (Shakespeare), 1, 2
Harlow, D., 119n30, 121n46

Harrison, John, 90
Harrison, Tony, 87–8
Hayden, Robert, 85
Heath, Malcolm, 69
Hecuba: and Achilles, 21, 68; and Agamemnon, 15–16, 27–8, 46–50, 55–60, 120n43; death of, 2, 21, 114n28; entrance of, 37–8; father of, 21, 22; in *Iliad*, 15, 21, 68; and Odysseus, 26, 38–42; rhetorical skills of, 31–3, 38–42, 45–51, 55–60; tomb of, 21, 29, 33, 58–60, 114n28, 124n31, 124n34; transformed into dog, 2, 21, 29, 31, 33, 43, 58–9, 124n31, n36, n40
Hecuba: modern performances of, 78–91; Renaissance views of, 1, 2, 29, 33, 69–72, 75
Hekate, 59, 114n28
Helen (Euripides), 21–2
Helen of Troy, 22, 39, 67; and Paris, 63–5, 80; and Polyxena, 26, 118n15; in *Trojan Women*, 127n8
Heracles, 42, 52, 67
Heracles (Euripides), 67
Hermogenes, 111n2
Herodotus, 49
hierosulia, 121n48. *See also* sacrilege
Higgins, Clare, 87
Hippolytus (Euripides), 25, 58, 67
Hogan, J. C., 118n17, 123n20
hosia (sacred rites), 46
hospitality, 4–6, 30–31, 36, 56–57, 74. *See also xenia*
human rights, 9–10, 75, 88
hypophora, 56

Iliad (Homer), 5, 39–41, 117n7; Hecuba in, 15, 21, 68; heroism in, 124n34; Neoptolemus in, 114n25; Odysseus in, 39; Polydorus in, 21–2; revenge in, 67, 68

Inferno (Dante), 3–4
Ion (Euripides), 67
Iphigenia, 16, 20
Iphigenia Among the Taurians (Euripides), 21–2
Iphigenia in Aulis (Euripides), 14, 42, 114n22; Renaissance views of, 71
Iraq War, 86–8, 90
Israeli-Palestinian conflict, 82

Jason, 58, 127n20
justice, 2, 6–8, 45, 48, 65, 69, 73; and *nomos*, 46–7, 56–7, 74; revenge as, 31, 57–9, 68, 72; self-help, 4, 7–10, 28, 30, 32, 51–60; Greek views of, 65, 68; in performances of *Hecuba*, 82–5. *See also dikê*

Kastely, James L., 31, 32, 119n26
Kent, Jonathan, 86–7
Kerrigan, John, 73
Khalaf, Lamis, 81–2
Kovacs, D., 116n19, 124n34
Kynossema. *See* Cynossema

laws, 50–1, 57, 112n12; traditional, 6–7, 32, 74; unwritten, 4–5, 8–9, 30–1. *See also nomos*
Lemnian women, 9, 51
Libanius, 111n2
Linklater, Kristin, 89
Lippard, Alex, 89
Lister, Henry Bertram, 78
Lloyd, M., 117n11
Longinus, 16
Lotti, Antonio, 77
Lucian, 111n2
Lumley, Jane, 71
Lysias, 50

marriage, 20, 44, 79; and concubines, 49–50; and gender roles, 121n46; of Neoptolemus, 113n18

Matthaei, L. E., 118n19
Maurizio, Liza, 90
McDonald, Marianne, 90
McGuinness, Frank, 86–7
McLeish, Kenneth, 88–9
Medea (Euripides), 52, 58, 81; Renaissance views of, 71; as revenge tragedy, 67
Melian debate, 6
Memory of Salt, The (play), 90
Mercier, C. E., 120n43
Meridor, R., 116n18, 125n40
Metcalfe, Cranstoun, 77
Minotis, Alexis, 90
Mitchell, Ann, 89
Mitchell-Boyask, R., 119n26
monody, 54
Mossman, Judith, 31–2, 38, 45, 68–9
Murphy, Fionnuala, 86–7
mythopoiesis, 14–23, 30, 39
Mytilenean debate, 6

Nelson, Jennifer, 85
Nelson, Marilyn, 85
Neoptolemus, 1; and Polydorus, 114n25; and Polyxena, 16–20, 43; and pyrrhic dance, 113n19; wedding of, 113n18
Nikander of Colophon, 114n28
9/11 attacks, 9
Niobe, 44
nomos (law), 30, 31, 39, 50, 115n5; of burial, 59; and justice, 46–7, 56–7, 74; and *nomitomen,* 40; and *peithô,* 57. *See also* laws

odes, choral, 26–8, 34, 43, 61–5
Odysseus, 21; on barbarians, 40, 41, 56; in *Iliad,* 39; morality of, 118n17; and Polyxena, 25–6; rhetoric of, 26, 37–41
Odyssey (Homer), 5, 39; Cyclops in, 14, 53; revenge in, 67
Oedipus Tyrannos (Sophocles), 29, 30, 32, 49, 53, 58
operatic adaptations, 77
Orel, Gwen, 89
Orestes (Euripides), 3, 22–23, 67, 111nn4–5
Orion, 53
Ovid, 3, 59, 70–1

Pacuvius, 114n21
Palestinian-Israeli conflict, 82
Paris, 63–5, 80
Patroclus, 16, 113n19
Paxinou, Katina, 90
peithô (persuasion), 31, 47, 57, 120n44. *See also* rhetoric
Peloponnesian War, 4, 6, 22, 74
Pentheus, 53
peplos (robe), 17, 62, 125n4
Pericles, 4, 41, 49, 112n14
Perloff, Carey, 82–5
Persian Wars, 22, 35, 49, 53
persuasion. *See peithô*
Phaedra, 58
philia (friendship), 32, 48, 56–7, 118n17; aristocratic, 6; reciprocity in, 50; and *xenia,* 56–7, 123n21
philos (friend), 38–9
Phoenician Women (Euripides), 3, 74, 111n5; papyri of, 111n4; Renaissance views of, 71; revenge in, 67; sacrifice in, 42
Pindar, 47
pity, 6, 8, 38–43, 47–8, 54, 75, 78; and rhetoric, 55; Zeitlin on, 117n26; tragic pity, 72–3. *See also* supplication
Plato, 68
Plutarch, 3, 112nn14–15
Polydorus, 6, 20–1, 27, 30, 36; corpse of, 5, 52, 63; ghost of, 5, 13, 25, 35–6; in *Iliad,* 21–2; and Neoptolemus, 114n25
Polygnotus (painter), 16
Polymestor, 21, 28, 51–60; and Agamemnon, 116n18; children

of, 30, 32, 46, 52–3; as Greek ally, 22, 27, 48, 54, 123nn20–21; prophecies of, 23, 29, 58–9; rhetoric of, 55–6
Polyxena, 26–7, 36, 38; and Achilles, 20, 44, 79, 117n6; in art, 16–19, 114n20; as *geras*, 35, 37, 117n6; and Neoptolemus, 16–20, 43; and Odysseus, 25–6; sacrifice of, 16–20, 42–5, 118n15, 119nn24–32; Sophocles' play about, 16, 34
politics of the late 5thcentury BCE, 4, 34, 37, 41
powerful versus powerless, 10, 30–1, 34, 38, 41, 44, 46, 76, 86, 111n10, 119n26
Priam (king of Troy), 1, 15, 21, 114n20
Protagoras, 68
pyrrhic dance, 18, 113n19

Quintus of Smyrna, 3, 114n21, 114n28

Rabelais, François, 126n9
Rabinowitz, Nancy, 44–5
rape, 16, 50, 121n51
reciprocity. *See charis*
Redgrave, Vanessa, 87–8
Renaissance theater, 1, 2, 29, 33, 35, 69–72, 77, 126n17
revenge, 25, 51–4; Aristotle on, 69; Bacon on, 125n40; and gender roles, 32, 51, 126n17; as justice, 31, 57–9, 68, 72; Kovacs on, 124n34; language of, 7, 116n20; Reckford on, 121n5; Shakespeare on, 2; and vendetta, 8, 68, 116n19
revenge tragedy, 3, 35, 67–73, 75, 85, 126n17; Crane on, 79–80; Kerrigan on, 73
rhetoric, 12, 30, 73; Aristotle on, 3, 68; Hecuba's use of, 26–8, 31–3, 38–42, 45–51, 55–60, 120n38, 123n24; Odysseus' use of, 26, 37–41; *peithô* and, 47, 57, 120n44; Polymestor's use of, 55–6; in performances, 78, 85, 89; Sophist, 21, 30, 39, 46–7. *See also agôn*
Rose, C. B., 113nn18–19
Royal Shakespeare Company, 87–8

Sack of Troy, 16
sacrifice, 16, 40–2; of Iphigenia, 16, 20, 42; of Polyxena, 16–20, 42–5, 84, 118n15, 119nn24–32; Thalmann on, 114n23
sacrilege, 46, 79, 121n48
Sands, Mick, 88, 89
Sato, Sachi, 90
satyr plays, 13–14, 53
Scaliger, J. C., 71, 126n14
Schlegel, Johann Elias, 77
Scodel, Ruth, 45, 119n28
Segal, C., 112n12
Seneca, 3, 67, 70, 77, 79, 114n21
September 11 attacks, 9
setting of *Hecuba*, 1, 13, 21–2
Shakespeare, William, 1, 2
Simonides, 16
skênê, 12, 13, 36, 117n2
slavery, 2, 26–7, 36, 40–2, 47, 121n2; as theme in modern productions, 84–6
slaves, 30–1, 33, 38, 42, 46, 51, 61–2; and concubines, 49–50, 121n51, 125n4; "rights" of, 8–9, 39, 116n18; Thracian, 22
Sophists, 21, 30, 39, 46–47. *See also* rhetoric
Sophocles, 14, 29, 71; *Ajax*, 5, 40, 49, 50, 74; *Antigone*, 5, 58, 71, 74; *Electra*, 71, 79; *Oedipus Tyrannos*, 29, 30, 32, 49, 53, 58; *Polyxena*, 16, 35
Stanton, G. R., 123n21
Strabo, 111n2
Suppliant Women (Euripides), 5, 74

supplication, 120n43; of Agamemnon by Hecuba, 27–8, 46–50, 123n43; of Odysseus by Hecuba, 26, 38–42; and women, 74, 84. *See also* pity
Sydney, Philip, 71

Talthybius, 13, 26, 34, 43
Teiresias, 58
Thalmann, W., 114n23, 124n32
Theseus, 37
Thucydides, 10, 68; on imperialism, 112n10; on Peloponnesian War, 4–7, 22
Timiades Painter, the, 16–17
timôria. See revenge
Tokyo Amateur Dramatic Club, 79
Troades (Seneca), 3, 70, 77, 79, 114n21
Trojan Women (Euripides), 3, 70, 78; Cassandra in, 15, 21, 49–50; Helen in, 127n8; modern performances of, 78; Renaissance views of, 71; revenge in, 67

Unforgiven (film), 72
unities, dramatic, 29–30, 33–4, 71, 72, 115n5

Valpy, Richard, 77
vendetta, 8, 68, 116n19. *See also* revenge
Vergil, 70, 114n21
Vietnam War, 75
vigilante films, 72

Walker, Kathryn, 90
Wertenbaker, Timberlake, 82, 90
West, Richard, 77
winds, 48, 51, 57–9, 62, 84, 117n8, 119n26, 123n27
women, 53, 55, 58, 61, 75, 82, 113n8, 116n22; Lemnian, 9, 51; rape of, 16, 50, 121n51; "rights" of, 8–9; traditional views of, 8, 28, 44, 112n14–15; morality of, 7, 74–5. *See also* gender roles
Workshop 360, 90

Xanthippus, 49
xenia (guest friendship), 27, 30, 46; and *philia*, 56–7, 123n21
Xerxes, 53

Zane, L., 90
Zeitlin, Froma, 74, 117n26, 120n44, 124n31
Zenobius, 22

 www.ingramcontent.com/pod-product-compliance
Ingram Content Group UK Ltd.
Pitfield, Milton Keynes, MK11 3LW, UK
UKHW022011220326
469246UK00006B/30